ULTIMATE
PUPPY TRAINING
FOR KIDS

ULTIMATE
PUPPY TRAINING
FOR KIDS

A Step-by-Step Guide for Exercises and Tricks

MARK VAN WYE, CEO OF
ZOOM ROOM
DOG TRAINING

ROCKRIDGE
PRESS

Interior and Cover Designer: Julie Schrader
Art Producer: Michael Hardgrove
Editor: Arturo Conde
Production Editor: Jenna Dutton
Custom Illustrations © 2020 Kate Francis
Interior art used under license from © iStockphoto.com, Shutterstock.com & Stocksy.com

ISBN: Print 978-1-64611-865-6 | eBook 978-1-64611-866-3
R0

To all of our incredible and passionate
Zoom Room trainers

CONTENTS

INTRODUCTION (FOR GROWN-UPS)

Thank you for taking this important step of including the kid or kids in your home in the shared journey of raising and training a puppy. We have found that one of the best recipes for success is getting everyone in the household on the same page, and we hope this book will help with that mission.

This book is intended for 8- to 12-year-olds. If you have younger children, it would be great to read the book aloud to them; however, the activities in this book are not recommended for younger kids. Most puppies will view 8- to 12-year-olds as people, but they'll view younger children as fellow puppies. That could mean chasing, wrestling, nipping, biting, and other behaviors that are normal for puppy-to-puppy interactions, but potentially dangerous to small children.

The goal of this book is for children to develop a deep understanding of their puppy's needs and drives and to provide the children with helpful suggestions and activities to deepen the bonds of communication. This can be a great boon to you, as having a child well-versed in puppy behavior gives you an extra set of eyes and ears around the home to report to you when they notice anything in need of attention.

But this is not a stand-alone puppy training book. We highly recommend that you, the grown-up, are the one actually responsible for your puppy's basic training, even if you got your puppy as a gift for your child with the understanding that they are going to be "responsible" for the puppy. We believe kids ages 8 and up can and should have important jobs around the home with regard to puppy care, but they shouldn't tackle this all on their own.

If you haven't already, we recommend that you get a copy of our companion book, *Puppy Training in 7 Easy Steps: Everything You Need to Know to Raise the Perfect Dog*, which *is* intended to be a comprehensive puppy training guide.

The activities and games in this volume are a complement to that book and provide many opportunities for children to assist in the raising of your new puppy.

Lastly, even though we think 8- to 12-year-olds make excellent trainers, there is always some degree of risk involved. Throughout the book, we will recommend that kids ask a grown-up for supervision or assistance. Accidents can happen, and when they do happen, they happen *fast*.

INTRODUCTION (FOR KIDS)

My name is Mark. I have a son, Meyer, who, as I write this book, is turning 10 years old. He's grown up with our own dog, a komondor named Clyde, but he's also been around lots and lots of other dogs and puppies–because I run the Zoom Room.

The Zoom Room is an indoor dog gym. We have trained more than 150,000 puppies and dogs. Well, that's not exactly right. You see, our motto is: *We don't train dogs. We train the people who love them.* What's so rewarding about what we do is that we focus on educating kids and grown-ups to really understand their pets. We teach people how to be amazing trainers.

That's important, because we don't follow you home or out on your adventures. *You* are the one who is going to be spending all that time with your puppy, so we believe it is important for you to understand how puppies think, why they do what they do, and how to fully welcome your new puppy to your family.

Throughout this book I'll be saying "we" because the ideas here come from all of us here at the Zoom Room. Our goal with this book is to help you become an especially knowledgeable and responsible companion to your puppy.

We hope you will enjoy it. And most of all: Congratulations on your new puppy!

WHO IS MY PUPPY?

Before you can train your puppy, you first have to understand them. Your puppy is your newest family member, but there's one huge difference between them and everyone else in your family: Your puppy is a totally different animal species!

There's a really big language barrier between you and your puppy, too. But we are here to help with that. Our hope is to teach you how to understand puppy language and to give you the tools you need to teach your puppy how to know what you are saying.

Understanding each other is the most important first step in this journey. This is the start of a beautiful friendship.

What Is It Like to Be a Puppy?

Everything in and around your home is brand new to your puppy. Your floor is new. The sound of your doorbell is new. The smell of food cooking in your kitchen is new. And you are new to your puppy, too!

Up until now, your puppy only knew their mother, their siblings, and a different home. Being away from them now is a bit uncomfortable. And while all of these new things are exciting for a puppy, they can also be scary.

You have a very important job in your puppy's life. Using patience and positivity, you will show your puppy what it means to feel safe and happy.

PREPARING FOR YOUR PUPPY

Chewing on stuff feels really good to puppies, and your puppy was born with this instinct to chew. But your puppy doesn't yet know which items they're allowed to chew. Puppy-proofing prepares your home to make it safe for your puppy. You can start by cleaning your bedroom.

1. Walk into your room and imagine seeing it with your puppy's eyes. All those toys and stuffed animals look a lot like their own chew toys, and you don't want to lose any of your special things to your puppy. Your socks and sneakers look especially delicious.

2. Move all of your toys, shoes, and anything else chewable out of your puppy's reach. Put them in bins, drawers, a chest, or put them in your closet. (Just make sure you don't accidentally lock your puppy in the closet. This happens!)

3. Now look at your room again. Does it look safe for your puppy and your stuff? Excellent. Except one thing is missing: What are you and your puppy going to play with?

4. Ask a grown-up for a puppy toy that you can keep in your room. It can be a rope toy, a puzzle or chew toy, or a stuffed and squeaky one. It can even be an empty plastic water bottle inside an old sock. If your puppy wants one of your toys, you can give them their own toy instead. It's a fair trade, and your puppy will love it.

Your Puppy's First Year

As you turn from 9 to 10, 10 to 11, and so on, of course you're still growing and changing. But these changes are pretty small if you compare them to your own first year on Earth. Back then, you were learning to crawl, take your first steps, speak, all those huge changes.

The same is true for your puppy. Year one is a biggie. Take a look at these important steps in a puppy's first year of life. But keep in mind that these time ranges aren't exact. Each puppy is unique. One thing they all have in common is that these changes happen really fast—your puppy is going to be a "teenager" in the blink of an eye!

PUPPY TIMELINE

BIRTH TO 18 MONTHS: PUPPY STAGE

This is a time for lots of socializing, training, and patience, as puppies have so much to learn. Crate training and potty training will begin right when your puppy joins your family. Basic obedience training and leash walking will come next.

BIRTH TO 4 MONTHS: PUPPY SOCIALIZATION PHASE

Starting with their mother and siblings, your puppy began learning how to get along with others. Now it's your turn. Give them lots of opportunities to meet new friends, especially during their first 16 weeks. When friends and family members come over, let them give your puppy treats.

2 TO 4 MONTHS: FIRST FEAR PHASE

Fear Phase? Well, that certainly sounds very scary, doesn't it? That's because it is. Any bad or frightening things that happen to a puppy during this period can cause them to have real problems as they get older. It is super important to do everything you can to make sure that all of their experiences are positive during this phase. You might notice your puppy being especially nervous or fearful. Keep them focused on the people, places, things, and activities that make them feel safe and happy.

2 TO 6 MONTHS: TEETHING

Your puppy will usually start to teethe and lose baby teeth around 2 months. By the time they're 6 months old, they should have all their grown-up teeth. Chew toys feel good in the mouth of a teething puppy.

6 TO 14 MONTHS: SECOND FEAR PHASE

The Second Fear Phase is usually only one month long, and it happens sometime between the ages of 6 months and 14 months. It's not as obvious as the First Fear Phase, but it's still really important to make sure their experiences are all positive. If you take your puppy to the dog park or out on an errand, be prepared to go back home if they seem anxious.

6 TO 18 MONTHS: ADOLESCENCE

Somewhere between the ages of six months and 18 months, your puppy will become a real teenager. You might notice that your puppy is a little less interested in playing with you and more interested in the rest of the world. They don't seem to listen as well as they used to. It's important to work on puppy training every day during this part of their life. If that seems like a lot of work, it isn't. Even two or three minutes of training each day makes a real difference.

Can My Puppy and I Be Friends?

You and your puppy are totally different species. Can the two of you really enjoy an interspecies friendship? Yes!

While you two have tons of differences, you have one very important thing in common. You are both domesticated species that come from wild ancestors. Domesticated is the opposite of wild.

What sets dogs apart from their wolf ancestors is how well they get along with humans. That works out perfectly for you. Friendship with this alien looks very promising indeed.

We know puppies developed in certain ways because of their fondness for people. But does that automatically make you friends? Nope. That's going to take some work, just like any friendship. So maybe the bigger question is: How do you become friends with anyone?

Being a friend—human or canine—requires three important ingredients:

1. You need to understand each other.

2. You need to enjoy doing stuff together.

3. You need to respect each other's boundaries.

We assume you are very excited to bond with your puppy. But how does your puppy feel? Do they want to play with you and be petted by you?

We're going to guess the answer is maybe, kind of, not sure. We're not being mean. We're just thinking about the First Fear Phase, and how you and everything in your home is still so new to your puppy.

That's why it's a good idea to begin with a fun game or activity that helps everyone get to know each other.

LET'S PLAY A GAME! TOUCH!

The first thing we want your puppy to learn is that being near you is pretty fantastic.

We're going to do this by teaching your puppy a little game called Touch. Every time your puppy touches you, they get rewarded. Be sure to ask a grown-up to supervise this game. Here's how to play:

1. Ask a grown-up for a treat pouch or a very small bag that you can clip to your left hip with a paper clip or binder clip.

2. Put about a dozen small meaty treats in the bag. You want very small pieces. If the pieces are kind of big, tear them into pieces not much bigger than a jelly bean.

3. Stick out your right hand in front of you and make a fist like you're waiting for a fist bump. This is called the Touch Stance.

4. Stand near your puppy and hold your fist down at the level of their chest, below their nose. Puppies like to smell anything near their face. Wait for your puppy to touch your hand with their nose. The moment your puppy touches your fist, say YES! in a very happy voice, and then with your left hand, take out a treat and give it to your puppy.

continued

5. Keep on playing for about two minutes or a dozen treats. Twelve touches in two minutes is perfect.

6. If your puppy doesn't touch your hand, try clapping your hands happily, then put out your fist. You can also try calling your puppy by name or making some kissy sounds. What you don't want to do is reach out and touch your puppy's nose. It's important that your puppy is the one doing the touching. Remember that if you are too far away from your puppy, their drive to sniff something near their face won't kick in, and if your hand is too close to their face, it will be too hard to tell who's touching whom.

7. If the game still isn't working, take one treat out of the bag with your left hand and bring it close enough to your puppy that they can smell it. Then put the treat back in the bag and get in the Touch Stance. At this point, your puppy should be pretty curious about the treat.

8. If the game is working, great! If it's just not happening, please don't feel frustrated. It could be that your puppy is tired or distracted. You can try again later when your puppy is in a more curious mood.

What Is My Puppy Saying?

Since part of being friends is understanding each other, let's learn to talk puppy by looking at canine body language.

Your puppy is talking to you all of the time. Not just with their voice—those barks, yips, squeaks, whines, and whimpers—but with their eyes, their spine, their ears, and that expressive tail.

Puppies learn through play, just like kids. Playing is the main way that puppies develop their social skills. Sometimes your puppy will lean down onto their elbows when they want to play with you. Other times your puppy will roll onto their back and show you their belly. That is your puppy telling you they want to be petted.

When your puppy is nervous or scared, you might see them put their tail between their legs or tremble. It is really important to tell a grown-up when your puppy shows you they are frightened. A grown-up can help you make your puppy feel safe again.

PUPPY PLAY GESTURES

Puppies use their tails, eyes, and whole bodies to talk to us. Your puppy can tell you lots of things with play gestures or motions. This is your puppy's way of telling you they are happy, excited, and feeling safe. Here are some classic puppy play gestures you are likely to see in your own puppy:

PLAY BOW	FLOPPY TAIL WAG
I want to play with you!	*Joy!*

RUB MY BELLY

I trust you. Pet me!

PUPPY EYES

I like you.

WAGGLE BOTTOM

I am so happy to see you!

LET'S PLAY A GAME! SCANVENGER HUNT

The best way to learn puppy language is to pay careful attention to your puppy's body language. Here is a game to remember what each gesture means.

1. On a piece of paper, write down the eight play gestures: Play Bow, Floppy Tail Wag, Rub My Belly, Puppy Eyes, Waggle Bottom, Goofy Face, Squint/Blink, and Huh.

2. Watch your puppy for an hour and see how many of the eight play gestures you see. Every time you see your puppy making one of these expressions, check it off.

3. Over the next week, keep it up, and see if you notice even more of them in your puppy's expressions. We bet you will get better at this game every day!

Between the ages of two months and four months, your puppy is in their First Fear Phase. Fear shows up as stress. Stress means you've been taken out of your place of comfort. If you see your puppy is stressed out, you should tell a grown-up. Together, you can take your puppy to a place that is familiar and comforting.

Here are some of the most important Signs of Stress to look out for. Remember that some of these signs could happen for reasons that don't involve fear or stress. But to be safe, always tell a grown-up.

HALF-MOON EYE

WHAT YOUR PUPPY FEELS:
I'm very nervous; please stay back.

WHAT YOUR PUPPY DOES:
Looks in another direction with the white of their eyes showing.

TAIL BETWEEN LEGS

WHAT YOUR PUPPY FEELS:
I'm frightened.

WHAT YOUR PUPPY DOES:
Cowers and tucks tail in between legs with little or no movement.

TREMBLING

WHAT YOUR PUPPY FEELS:
I'm in fight-or-flight mode. Please give me space.

WHAT YOUR PUPPY DOES:
Shivers or shakes body.

POINTY TAIL

WHAT YOUR PUPPY FEELS:
I'm not sure I like this.

WHAT YOUR PUPPY DOES:
Points tail out in line with the spine.

HIGH STIFF TAIL

WHAT YOUR PUPPY FEELS:
I'm nervous.

WHAT YOUR PUPPY DOES:
Points tail up high and stiff.

GROWLING

WHAT YOUR PUPPY FEELS:
Stay back, or I might bite you.

WHAT YOUR PUPPY DOES:
Purses lips forward; makes deep, low sounds.

YAWNING

WHAT YOUR PUPPY FEELS:
I'm stressed out.

WHAT YOUR PUPPY DOES:
Opens jaw wide, takes deep breath, sticks tongue out and acts tired.

SQUIRTING (PEEING)

WHAT YOUR PUPPY FEELS:
You're bigger than I am and stronger than I am.

WHAT YOUR PUPPY DOES:
Rolls on back and pees a little. Can also pee while crouching, tucking the tail, or exposing the belly.

RETREAT!

WHAT YOUR PUPPY FEELS:
I'm afraid. I want to get away.

WHAT YOUR PUPPY DOES:
Moves head and ears down, and leans back with weight on rear legs.

ALERT

WHAT YOUR PUPPY FEELS:
I am suspicious and alert.

WHAT YOUR PUPPY DOES:
Holds head high, cocks ears up and forward, furrows brow.

SNAPPING

WHAT YOUR PUPPY FEELS:
Back off!

WHAT YOUR PUPPY DOES:
Closes jaw suddenly to show teeth, like biting the air. Sometimes makes a snap or click sound.

VELCRO

WHAT YOUR PUPPY FEELS:
Please protect me. I'm scared.

WHAT YOUR PUPPY DOES:
Hugs against, between or behind you; leans full weight against your legs.

LICKING

WHAT YOUR PUPPY FEELS:
I'm nervous.

WHAT YOUR PUPPY DOES:
Uses tongue to lick lips or nose.

DRY SHAKE

WHAT YOUR PUPPY FEELS:
Something that happened recently really freaked me out, but I'm getting over it.

WHAT YOUR PUPPY DOES:
Shakes violently from side to side like a wet dog getting out of a bath.

DROOLING

WHAT YOUR PUPPY FEELS:
Maybe something smells delicious, but if there's no food around I may be feeling uneasy.

WHAT YOUR PUPPY DOES:
Saliva drips from the lower lip or jaw.

FIERCE

WHAT YOUR PUPPY FEELS:
Stay back!

WHAT YOUR PUPPY DOES:
Lowers head down, pulls ears back, leans weight forward on front legs.

Ask a Grown-Up

WHAT SHOULD YOU DO WHEN YOU SEE SIGNS OF STRESS? If at any time you happen to notice your puppy showing any Signs of Stress, be sure to tell a grown-up. Even better, see if you can sleuth out what might have caused the stress. Every time a creature experiences stress, there is always an *antecedent*. "Antecedent" simply means "a thing that came before."

If you notice your puppy trembling with tail between their legs, it's good to let a grown-up know. But if you *also* happen to notice that right before this happened, someone turned on the garbage disposal in the kitchen, that's even better. Maybe that sound was the antecedent—the thing that caused the fear response.

Just so you know, if that example were to actually happen, it doesn't mean your family would have to get rid of the garbage disposal. Not at all! This would be a job for *counter-conditioning*.

Counter-conditioning means teaching your puppy, using our example, that garbage disposals are wonderful creations, and that the sound they make is pure music. You can do this using positive training, treats, and taking things one little step at a time. We'll learn more about this in Chapter 3.

How Can I Communicate with My Puppy?

Now that you are beginning to understand your puppy, you might notice that they still don't know any human words. But that doesn't mean that your puppy can't understand you at all. Remember, puppies are domesticated, and they developed that way because of their love for humans.

So, even at birth, your puppy actually *does* already understand some of your body language and the tone of your voice. Puppies don't have to be taught when a human is happy or angry. They know this instinctively.

Your job is to make sure your puppy finds the world to be a wonderful, joyful place. Yelling, anger, and even pouting are emotional expressions your puppy will pick up on. We can't say enough how important it is to stay happy, patient, and positive.

CLAPPING: There's another cool thing puppies are born knowing: clapping. Most animals tend to run away from any kind of loud, banging sounds. If you see a deer or a squirrel, clap your hands and watch what happens. But puppies will instinctively come toward the sound of hand clapping or thigh slapping. (Fun fact: Horses do, too!)

KEEP IT SIMPLE: Don't confuse your puppy by using different training commands to mean the same thing. Everyone in your family should use the same training words with your puppy. If your puppy is going to learn the Down command, then everyone should use that same word: Down. Not "Lie down," or "Downward dog!" or "Down, boy."

JUST SAY IT ONCE: It's equally important not to repeat a word if your puppy didn't understand it the first time. If you say, "Down . . . down. Down. Down. Down!" before your puppy lies down, they are going to think that the command for Down is "Down down." This takes patience. But you can do it.

LET'S PLAY A GAME! THE NAME GAME

For this game, you're going to teach your puppy their name. You will want to keep it simple, avoid repeating yourself, and be positive and upbeat. Everyone in your family should call your puppy by the same name. No nicknames! You can use funny nicknames when your puppy is older.

For a lot of puppy training, you want to be in a quiet place. But for this game, you actually want to be somewhere that's a little distracting.

If you have a fenced yard outside, that will work. If not, you should ask a friend or family member to help by hanging out in another room and making some noises from time to time.

Why do we want your puppy distracted? In this game, your puppy will be rewarded every time they look at your face. In order to repeat the training several times, after looking at your face your puppy will need to look away at something else. Be sure to ask a grown-up to supervise during this game.

Here's how to play:

1. Put your puppy on a leash and hold one end of the leash. You might want to hold the leash about halfway. (This is called keeping your puppy on a short leash.)

2. Ask a grown-up for a treat pouch or small zip-top bag full of treats. Remember to use very small meaty treats.

3. Stand close enough to your puppy that you can reach out and touch their nose. If your puppy changes position, move closer so that their nose is within touching distance. Keep the leash short.

4. In a very happy voice, say your puppy's name. Say it only *once*.

5. If your puppy moves their head to look up at your face, exclaim YES! and then give your puppy a treat.

6. Repeat this game for about two minutes or a dozen treats. After each YES!, if your puppy isn't looking away from you, you need a better distraction. Remember, a distraction is anything that will grab your puppy's attention. Ask a family member to crinkle up some paper or make a silly sound.

continued

7. If the happy voice wasn't enough, here's how to get your puppy to look up at you: You will *lure* your puppy with a treat. Luring is when you use a treat to guide your puppy to do the behavior you want. Simply take out a treat and hold it near your puppy's nose. As soon as they sniff and notice it, raise the treat up toward your face as you happily speak your puppy's name one time.

8. Your puppy is very likely to follow the scent of the treat up toward your face with their gaze. As soon as your puppy turns their head toward your face, exclaim YES! and give them the treat.

9. Try again, this time without the treat luring. Did it work? If so, keep on going for about five minutes or a dozen treats. If it didn't work, don't give up. Remember: Don't repeat their name more than once, and stay patient. Hold another treat by your puppy's nose and move the treat toward your face a little more slowly this time as you speak your puppy's name. You can try making your voice a little higher and happier, too.

10. By now, your puppy should be really good at turning to look at you whenever you say their name. If not, it could be that the treats you're using aren't tasty enough. In Chapter 3, we're going to talk about what kinds of treats are the best ones for training.

TIP It is extremely important never to use your hands to guide your puppy into the correct position. If you need to show your puppy what you want them to do, use a treat to lure them.

How Do I Make My Puppy Happy?

You and your puppy are now beginning to speak the same language. That is excellent. We need just two more ingredients to form a lifelong friendship: doing stuff together and respecting each other's space. That's what this section is all about.

PHYSICAL INTERACTIONS

Let's look at what kinds of touch your puppy likes and doesn't like. When you pet your puppy, pay attention to how they respond. You can tell how they're feeling by looking at their body language. You want to see Goofy Face, Floppy Tail, Squint/Blink, Rub My Belly, or Puppy Eyes. These all let you know you're making your puppy feel blissful.

If your puppy gets all wound up and starts darting around or doing a Play Bow, they're telling you they'd rather play a game with you than be petted.

It's just as important to know what kinds of touch to avoid. Don't sit or lie on top of your puppy or try to ride them around. Don't stick your finger in their ears or mouth. Avoid greeting them face-to-face—humans greet this way, but puppies do not.

As hard as it might be, don't give your puppy a hug. Most puppies do not like to be hugged. Instead, try scratching them behind the ears—they love that so much as it is a hard place for them to reach.

PLAYING GAMES

Puppies are playful creatures, and you can delight your puppy by playing games with them.

However, not all games are created the same. For example, chase games are not a good idea. It's true that puppies love to chase and be chased. But it's also true that chasing you around can quickly spark your puppy's prey drive. You want your puppy to see you as their loving buddy, not as prey.

What about the other way around? Is it okay for you to do the chasing?

Chasing your puppy is also not a good idea, but for a totally different reason. Your puppy will enjoy it, but let them play this game with other dogs. If you chase your puppy, you will teach them that it's a good thing to run away from you. We want your puppy to always come toward you.

Luckily, there are many wonderful games and training activities you two can enjoy together.

LET'S PLAY A GAME! FETCH!

Fetch plays off your puppy's love of chasing things. It might seem pretty simple, but the little details count. Sure, you toss a ball, and your puppy chases after it, gets it, and brings it back.

But then what? Now your puppy is standing in front of you with a slobbery ball in their mouth. And if you ask your puppy, this game is not at all over. Here's the best way to play Fetch!

1. You'll need two balls or throwing items. You can use tennis balls, flying discs, or any other dog toys made for fetching.

2. Your puppy should be off leash, so a fenced yard is best. If a grown-up says it's okay, you can play indoors.

3. Throw the toy.

4. When your puppy brings it back to you, give them lots of praise, but do *not* take the toy from your puppy's mouth.

5. Instead, pull out the second ball or toy and show it to your puppy.

6. Most puppies will drop the first ball when they see the second one. If your puppy drops the one in their mouth, say DROP! and then toss the second one.

7. While your puppy chases the second one, pick up the first one.

8. If your puppy doesn't drop the first toy, go ahead and toss the second one. Your puppy will probably be so excited to chase it that they'll drop the first one. When they do drop it, say DROP!

9. Repeat steps 4 to 8 until your puppy is tired of this game.

Not every puppy likes to play Fetch. Some will do it once or twice and then get bored. Others could play this game until midnight and never tire. Either way, when you play Fetch, you are also getting to know your puppy and learning what they like.

WHAT DOES
MY PUPPY NEED?

Puppies don't come with instruction manuals. But we think it's exciting to understand how your puppy behaves, and it's really important to know what they need. Let's explore how they sleep, eat, go potty, exercise, and play.

Your puppy is growing up very quickly. They will need lots of rest and just the right amount of healthy food to help them grow. Exercise and playtime keep your puppy's mind and body challenged and fit.

By helping your puppy learn where they will sleep, where they should and shouldn't go potty, and providing them plenty of opportunities for fun, games, and running around, you are setting them up for success as the happy, healthy, well-behaved dog they will soon become.

You can think of this chapter as your puppy's missing manual!

Where Does My Puppy Sleep?

At night, your puppy will have a bedtime, just like you. But during the day, your puppy will nap a lot—sometimes as much as 20 hours a day!

NAP TIME: When your puppy naps, always leave them be. There will be times when they need to wake up to go potty or move to the crate, though. If you do need to wake your puppy, remember to always use your voice and never your hands.

WHY DOES MY PUPPY SLEEP IN THE CRATE? Dogs are den animals, just like their wolf ancestors. The great-great-great-great-grandparents of your puppy went to sleep at night in safe spaces like caves, all piled on top of each other. Your puppy enjoys enclosed spaces, too, like being underneath a table or a bed.

Your home is now your puppy's home, too. Your puppy also has their own special room: their crate. A crate might just look like a box with a sort of cage-looking door. This isn't at all how your puppy sees it. To your puppy, it's their cozy private fort. If your puppy has proper crate training, they will feel safe and cheerful there.

Crate Training Rules

As soon as you bring your puppy home, crate training begins. It's the grown-up's job to take care of crate training. This includes feeding your puppy their meals near and eventually inside the crate. It also means moving the crate to different places around your home. Ask a grown-up if you can help with any of these activities so you can learn more about crate training.

Again, this is your puppy's private fort. A lot of kids think it's fun to try to climb inside, but it's important to respect the crate as a place for puppies only. You should never knock, bang, or tap on the crate. (No shaking or wiggling the crate when your puppy is inside, either.)

Your puppy really does not want to have an accident in bed. And the number-one cause of this is putting a puppy in a crate that is too big. The crate should be big enough only for your puppy to turn around inside and lie down. If you ever notice that your puppy has had an accident in the crate, be sure to tell a grown-up.

LET'S TEACH YOUR PUPPY:
MAGIC CRATE

Before your puppy came to live with you and your family, they probably slept in a crate in their first home. If so, crate training will be pretty easy. But if not, it may take a little time for your puppy to fall in love with their home-within-your-home.

Let's help with a game of Magic Crate. You're going to have to be extra sneaky!

1. Hide a treat in your pocket. When your puppy isn't looking, quickly drop or toss a treat or a few treats into the crate. Your puppy will be delighted to find these surprises in there.

2. It's very important that your puppy not see you do this. If they see you, your puppy learns that you are the wonderful person giving them a treat, and the crate just happens to be the place where you threw it. The trick is to make your puppy think that the crate is magical. You're not giving puppy a treat. The *crate* is doing it!

3. Don't worry if your puppy doesn't go directly to the treats. Don't try to lure your puppy over. Think of the treats like hidden surprises to discover later. Your puppy is naturally curious and will eventually sniff around the crate and be overjoyed that their magic crate makes goodies.

4. You can hide treats in the crate during the day. It is especially important to do this during your puppy's first week at home. It helps them see the crate as a happy place. But remember to be sneaky and don't let your puppy see you tossing in the treats!

What Does My Puppy Eat?

Dogs are *omnivores*. That means they eat everything: all kinds of meat, as well as vegetables, fruits, and grains. But not all omnivores are alike. Some omnivores like to eat more vegetables than meat or the other way around. Your puppy likes meat the best.

For their first six months, your puppy will eat three to four meals each day. They have their own special food and should not eat table scraps. People food doesn't have all the nutrients puppies need to grow big, strong, and healthy. Giving them your food also creates bad manners like begging.

Your puppy may beg for more food after they finish their meal. Ignore this. Your puppy isn't actually hungry. They just *think* they want more because dogs are scavenger animals. This is because their ancestors never knew when or where their next meal might come from. They had to eat whatever scraps they could find. Now your puppy thinks it needs to do the same. Overfeeding is also very unhealthy for puppies and will cause them to gain too much weight.

SAFETY AROUND PUPPIES AND THEIR FOOD

Give your puppy space during mealtime and never take away their food. When you learned the Fetch game, we talked about how dangerous it is to try to take away a dog's toy. If you take away a dog's food while they're eating, you could get seriously bitten—even by your own puppy.

LET'S TEACH YOUR PUPPY: GENTLE

In this activity you will hand-feed your puppy their meal to teach the Gentle command. It is very important that a grown-up supervise.

It is very important for your puppy to bond with you and everyone in your home. Hand-feeding your puppy their entire meal is a wonderful way to help build trust.

You also need to know how to give your puppy a treat without fear of being nipped. And your puppy needs to know how to gently take a treat from your hand without nipping you.

1. Wait until it is your puppy's mealtime. Have a grown-up measure out your puppy's meal into a small container you will hold—anything other than the dog food bowl your puppy normally uses. You probably feed your puppy kibble, but if it's wet food, you can still do this activity. Just use about 25 tiny treats instead.

2. Sit in a chair near the place where your puppy normally eats.

3. Keep your fingers all together so that your hand looks like a mitten. With your palm facing up toward the ceiling, stretch your hand out completely flat like a plate. Now place one piece of kibble in your hand.

4. Lower your hand to just at or below your puppy's nose level. If your puppy gently takes the piece of kibble from your hand with their mouth, say GENTLE, in a calm voice. This is how your puppy learns that the word "gentle" means eating this way.

5. If your puppy opens their mouth too widely or seems like they're overexcited and might nip your fingers, say AH AH in a firm but not angry voice as you quickly close your hand into a fist around the kibble and lift it all the way out of their reach. We'll talk more about AH AH in chapter 3. It is how you tell your puppy, "Sorry, that's not the answer I was looking for."

6. Now go back and repeat steps 3 through 5. Your puppy really wants to eat, so they will learn this command very quickly. It should only take a few tries before you are saying GENTLE with every piece of kibble.

7. Keep going until your puppy has eaten their entire meal.

Where Does My Puppy Potty?

Puppies have an incredible ability to smell. They can easily recognize the smell of dog urine. So when it is potty time, they love to pee in the same place every time, or to go where another dog has gone.

Puppy bodies hold urine in the same place human bodies do: the bladder. Your puppy is still very young, so the muscles in their bladder aren't very strong yet. When you have to pee, it's those muscles that allow you to "hold it in" until you can get to a bathroom.

A puppy can hold it in for about one hour for every month of age. So a one-month-old puppy can hold their pee for about one hour, a two-month-old puppy can wait two hours, and then longer as they get older.

By the time they are six months old—and often earlier—they'll be able to sleep through the night without having to go out and potty.

PREVENTING ACCIDENTS

While your puppy can hold it in for an hour or longer, depending on age, they can't tell time. But luckily, you can. So when it's potty time, grab the leash and a grown-up and head to the potty place.

Your puppy will also *tell* you when they really have to go. A puppy who has to go potty may sniff the ground as they walk around in circles, sometimes arching their back. They may also go into a corner, look all around, or whine for no obvious reason. So be on the lookout for any of these signs that your puppy may need to go potty.

WHAT TO DO WHEN ACCIDENTS HAPPEN

If your puppy goes to the bathroom inside, never scold them. Even if you are feeling frustrated that there's now a mess to clean up, don't let your puppy see that you are upset.

Tell a grown-up instead. Remember how we said puppies like to go potty where they smell pee? The mess needs to be cleaned up right away.

If you catch your puppy having an accident, they may still need to go to the bathroom some more. Leave the mess for now and quickly take your puppy outside to their potty place.

Stay there for a few minutes. This will give your puppy a chance to finish. Then you should praise your puppy and hand out a treat.

Even if they don't have to go, taking them outside helps them learn that this is their potty place.

LET'S TEACH YOUR PUPPY:
WHAT TO DO AT THE POTTY PLACE

Your family should decide on a potty place, somewhere outside and close by because puppies can't hold it in for very long.

1. When you take your puppy to the potty place, always go with a grown-up and bring treats.

2. Always keep your puppy on leash. Even in a fenced-in yard, the leash is needed to keep your puppy from getting distracted. It helps your puppy focus on going potty.

3. Don't pull or tug on the leash. Keep it nice and loose, which means sticking close to your puppy.

4. Be patient. It may take a few minutes for a puppy to go. After ten minutes, if they still haven't gone, head back inside and try again later.

5. When your puppy succeeds in going potty in the potty place, warmly praise them and give them a treat.

6. Offer to help with clean-up. Your puppy doesn't care who picks up after them, but your grown-up will appreciate your help.

7. Head back inside, grab some toys, and play together for a little while. This playtime is an extra reward for a potty job well done.

RING THE POTTY BELL

You've learned some signs that let you know your puppy needs to go potty, but wouldn't it be nice if your puppy could just tell you, "Hey, I gotta go"?

Your wish is granted! Except your puppy will ring a bell instead of speaking. You're going to train your puppy to ring a bell when they need to go potty.

Ask a grown-up to buy a hand bell and to supervise this activity. You will also need a pouch or bag filled with plenty of treats and a long piece of fabric.

1. Remember the Touch exercise? (See page 7.) You're going to do almost the same thing here, except instead of holding out your hand for puppy to touch with their nose, hold out the bell.

2. When your puppy touches the bell with their nose, exclaim YES! and, with your other hand, give the puppy a treat.

3. If your puppy shies away, you can attract them. With your other hand, hold a treat near your puppy's nose and bring the treat slowly toward the bell. Be sure to wait for the exact moment your puppy's nose touches the bell to say YES!

4. Repeat this about a dozen times so that your puppy has no problem at all touching the bell with their nose for a treat.

5. Now take a few steps away. If your puppy follows you, ask the grown-up to help by gently holding the puppy's collar. Hold out the bell. The grown-up should release the collar. Your puppy now has to walk over a few steps and touch the bell with their nose. Say YES! and give a treat with your other hand.

6. Repeat this about a dozen times. Now your puppy will walk toward the bell and touch it with their nose to get a treat.

7. Next, you will tie one end of the fabric around the handle of the bell. Tie the other end around the doorknob of the door where you want your puppy to go out to go potty. The bell should be right at the height of your puppy's nose. (When your puppy gets taller, shorten the fabric so that the bell always hangs at nose height.)

8. You're right back at Step 5, except now the bell is tied to the fabric. You should stand right by the door while the grown-up holds your puppy by the collar several feet away. When the grown-up releases the collar, your puppy should approach the bell and touch it with their nose. Cheerfully say YES! and give a treat.

9. If your puppy is not going for it, try luring or have the grown-up move them closer to the door. Once your puppy has no problem going over to touch the bell, you're ready to move on to the next step.

10. Place your puppy's leash on a table or on the floor. Repeat step 9, but instead of giving puppy a treat, say YES! Then put the leash on your puppy's collar, open the door, and head to the usual potty place. When your puppy goes to the bathroom, give them tons of praise and a treat, and then head back inside to celebrate.

11. At this point, you might think you're all done. But your puppy has only learned to ring a bell when they want to go *outside*. Outside can mean potty, but it can also mean going outside to play. Here's how we teach your puppy it's a *Potty* Bell, not a Play Bell:

12. If your puppy doesn't go potty when you take them out, head right back inside. You're not punishing your puppy. You're simply not giving them the reward they had hoped for.

13. Inside, take the leash off. This is called resetting. When you reset, you're starting the training over at the beginning. You will want to wait a while before trying again since your puppy doesn't actually need to go potty.

continued

14. Later, when you're pretty sure your puppy really does have to go potty, try again. Stand near the door with the leash. The grown-up doesn't have to hold the collar. See if your puppy approaches the bell on their own. If not, encourage your puppy to ring the bell by luring with a treat.

15. When your puppy rings the bell, put their leash on, and head outside to the potty place. Give your puppy a few minutes. If your puppy does go to the bathroom, give them lots of praise and a treat before you return home. If the puppy doesn't go to the bathroom, go back to step 11.

Remember to use very small treats and to practice this a few times a day, every day, until your puppy has perfected the ringing of the Potty Bell. Puppies cannot pay attention for a long time, so you should make sure each training session is only 15 to 20 minutes long.

Why Does My Puppy Need to Walk?

A tired dog is a happy dog. Giving your puppy plenty of exercise every day will not only make them happy but also healthy and better behaved.

What counts as exercise? Until your puppy is fully vaccinated around the age of four months, you'll need to stick to playing inside, running around your own yard if you have an enclosed one, or visiting a safe puppy place like Zoom Room, if there's one nearby.

A puppy can walk about a mile a day for every month old they are. But taking a two-month-old puppy on a two-mile walk is far too long. Puppies need lots of little walks. Three or four short walks are much better than one long one for a puppy of any age..

TAKING YOUR PUPPY FOR A WALK

When you first take your puppy for walks, you're asking your puppy to do a lot of things that don't really make sense to them. They need to wear a collar, a harness, and be attached to a leash. That can feel pretty weird for your puppy. But you can fix that!

GET YOUR PUPPY USED TO WEARING THEIR COLLAR. Your puppy needs to always wear their collar. It is important because it has an ID tag with your puppy's name and your phone number if your puppy is ever lost. The collar is also important when your puppy has to go potty. During potty breaks, you'll attach a leash to the collar to save time. Your puppy is not used to their collar yet, so they may try to paw at it. Simply ignore this.

GET YOUR PUPPY USED TO BEING ON LEASH. You will use a piece of equipment called a *house line* to help your puppy get used to being on leash. It looks like a normal leash except it doesn't have a handle, and it is a little thinner. Your puppy will wander around indoors wearing it, dragging the line behind them. We use a house line for this because it is thinner and lighter than a regular leash. It lets your puppy walk normally, and there is no chance it could get stuck on something and yank your puppy.

GET YOUR PUPPY USED TO WEARING A FRONT-CLIP HARNESS. Once your puppy is used to the collar, house line, and leash, it is time for the front-clip harness. Why do you need one? If your puppy pulls on the leash and you pull the other way, your puppy will just pull harder—it's called an *oppositional reflex*. But when you attach the leash to their chest, if your puppy sees a squirrel and tries to chase it, the harness will turn your puppy around so that they are now facing you. Puppies learn to walk politely on a front-clip harness a lot better than they do when the leash is attached to their collar or back. Make sure to take the harness off your puppy when you are in your house.

LET'S TEACH YOUR PUPPY:
STICK BY ME

Let's play a game with your puppy and the house line. Select the room in your home with the most space. You're going to be walking backward, so ask a grown-up to help you move furniture out of the way. You can also play this game in a fenced yard.

Only use a real house line, and never leave the house line on your puppy when your family leaves home.

1. Get a bag filled with treats, the house line, and go to the open space.

2. Now you dance! Start dancing around, always walking *backward*. Travel back away from your puppy while calling them over to you. There's no command, so you can say, "Come on! Over here! Yay!" and keep the tone upbeat and happy. You can also clap your hands, slap your thighs, and whistle.

3. Whenever your puppy comes near you, give them a treat.

4. Keep moving. Be sure to always face your puppy and travel backward. You can probably guess why, right? If you turned your back and started running, that would be chasing. Remember never to encourage your puppy to chase you.

5. Keep playing for about five minutes, always trying to put some distance between you and your puppy, then allowing them to come to you for a treat and praise. The point of this game is for your puppy to discover there is a magical three-foot bubble space around you, and that whenever they enter this space, great things happen.

6. Once your puppy has mastered this game, pick up the loose end of the house line and hold it. Keep playing the game, exactly as before, except now your puppy will be following you around *on leash*. The leash should always be loose. Never pull your puppy toward you. Use your voice, treats, and clapping instead. Keep playing for about another five minutes.

continued

Stick By Me continued

7. me a few times a day until your puppy always comes into your three-foot bubble space. Three feet is best because the normal leash you use is six feet long. Your leash will always be loose if your puppy stays within the bubble space.

TIPS AND TROUBLESHOOTING

YANKING: Don't yank on the leash or drag your puppy. It will make your puppy very unhappy.

There is also a scientific reason why you shouldn't tug on the leash. Remember the *oppositional reflex* (page 34)? A reflex is something your body does automatically, and oppositional means opposite, like in the opposite direction. Your puppy has this natural response and so do you. Let's say your goal is to walk your puppy from the corner to the door. If you tug on the leash toward the door, your puppy will pull the other way. They're not trying to be difficult. It's a reflex.

SO HOW DO YOU GET YOUR PUPPY TO WALK WHERE YOU WANT THEM TO GO? You should call your puppy by their name in a friendly voice, clap hands, or lure with a treat.

BOLTING: So much of the world is new to your puppy, and they want to explore. Anything could make your puppy want to run off. This is why you should have a grown-up with you on walks. You should not walk your puppy until a grown-up is sure you are big enough not to get accidentally pulled down by your puppy.

RUNNING AHEAD: When you go for a walk with your puppy and a grown-up, it is important that you stick together. If you run ahead, your puppy will want to run off, too. Keep working on the happy bubble space by sticking within three feet of your puppy.

Why Does My Puppy Need Friends?

As your puppy grows, you're going to want to take them out into the world to all your favorite places. Think how much fun it will be when your friends come over and play with your puppy. These activities will be delightful if your puppy is happy and well behaved.

If not, even a simple walk around the block with a fearful or stressed-out puppy can be rough.

The way to a well-behaved puppy is through *socialization*, and plenty of it. Socialization means exposing your puppy to new people, places, things, sounds, smells, dogs and other animals in a safe, controlled, and positive manner.

Your puppy needs socialization their whole life, but during their first four months, it is especially important.

HOW TO SOCIALIZE YOUR PUPPY ON WALKS

If you are out on a walk with your puppy and you meet a man with a beard, you might think nothing of this, but a beard is new to your puppy. And during a fear phase, new things might really be scary.

You can show your puppy that new things are nothing to be afraid of. The same goes for kids on skateboards, people wearing shorts, delivery people pushing a handcart, people in uniforms, and people in wheelchairs.

What you're going to need is some *counter-conditioning* and the help of a grown-up. Counter-conditioning means taking something that seems scary and making it a positive experience.

For example, let's say you, your grown-up, and your puppy meet a man with a beard when out for a walk. You or your grown-up should approach the man and ask him if he would be willing to give your puppy a treat.

If the man says yes, give him a treat to offer the puppy. Then, ask him to squat down a little and hold out his hand so your puppy can approach him and take the treat.

If your puppy wanders right over and takes the treat, that's a great sign! Praise your puppy. You can even give them an additional goody.

If your puppy hides behind your legs, barks, or shows any Signs of Stress, do not force it. Your puppy is scared, and this will only make the fear worse. Try again another day.

As soon as the next day, your puppy may be ready for another interaction like this. But always watch for those Signs of Stress.

Interacting with other dogs will help your puppy develop confidence and their own special style of play. Most important, your puppy will grow up to be easygoing and happy around other dogs.

Before your puppy is fully vaccinated, playing with adult dogs will have to wait. Even a healthy dog can be a danger to your puppy because adult dogs may have germs on their coat or paws.

RULES FOR MEETING NEW DOG FRIENDS

Whether it's a scheduled playdate, a chance meet-and-greet on the street, or a trip to the park, here are some helpful tips to remember:

1. DO NOT GIVE TREATS. Getting to play with other dogs is so rewarding to your puppy that you don't need to give your puppy any other kind of treat or reward.

2. OBSERVE BODY LANGUAGE. Watch for lots of Play Gestures. They're a sign that your puppy is having a fantastic time. But also look for the Signs of Stress. Dogs love to wrestle, and you might see some barking, growling, chasing, and tackling. All of this is okay as long as your puppy is still showing happy Play Gestures and not looking for a place to hide.

3. OFF-LEASH IS SAFER. You might think your puppy is always better off when they're on leash. At the dog park or on a playdate, leashes can actually get in the way and become tangled. Having both dogs on leashes often makes them greet face-to-face, which isn't the way dogs usually say hello.

4. WATCH FOR MISMATCHES. Every puppy has their own play style. Some dogs might really love to chase, but your puppy might not love being chased. If you see that another dog has too much energy for your puppy, and your puppy appears frightened or stressed out, tell a grown-up so they can help.

There are places like the Zoom Room that have safe puppy socialization classes and playgroups with same-age puppies. If there is one near you, it is a terrific activity for you and your puppy.

Once your puppy is fully vaccinated, you will have lots of opportunities for your puppy to meet other dogs during playdates with a friend's dog, while out on daily walks, or during visits to the dog park.

5. MAKE SURE THERE'S A SAFE SPACE. In case your puppy feels a little overwhelmed, they need a safe place to retreat to, like under a chair. A good hiding spot will let your puppy calm down while still watching the other dogs play. At some point, it may look like too much fun to resist, and your puppy will join back in the fun. But if your puppy is too scared to come out, don't force it. Put their leash on and head home. Tomorrow is another day.

6. UNDERSTAND THE PUPPY PASS. Adult dogs greet each other by sniffing each other's belly and bottom. They don't greet face-to-face. Your puppy is just learning this stuff. Your puppy might do some things that an older dog considers kind of rude, like face sniffing or nipping. Adult dogs are aware that your puppy is just a puppy. They will give your puppy what we call a "Puppy Pass," which means putting up with some behavior they would not allow from a grown-up dog. But a Puppy Pass only goes so far. If your puppy is taking things too far, the other dog might bark or swat. These are important lessons for your puppy to learn about boundaries.

7. END ON A HIGH NOTE. Whether at a playdate or the park, always try to end on a high note. You help your puppy socialize by leaving them with all positive memories of their playtime with other pups.

8. DON'T CALL YOUR DOG. When it's time to go, don't call your dog to come to you. Your puppy is having a great time and will probably ignore you. When you give a command, you want your puppy to do it. In this case, because your puppy likely won't come when you call, just walk over, put on the leash, and head back home.

TRAIN MY PUPPY!

t is time to learn how to train your puppy using positive rewards. Training is really the same as teaching. You will show your puppy what you would like them to do and then reward them when they succeed.

You will also learn how puppies learn. If you understand how a puppy sees the world, it will make you a better teacher.

Puppies need to repeat things many times in order to learn. That means to be a good trainer, you need to practice with your puppy often. But puppies also have short attention spans, so each training session should be very short.

Try to practice regularly with your puppy. For example, do a quick session when you get home from school, another when you finish your homework, and one more after dinner. On weekends, you could do five or six sessions each day. Each session only has to be around five minutes long.

What counts is doing things the same way each time, so make puppy training a new habit, and keep building upon your successes.

What Do I Need to Train My Puppy?

On the first day of school, you know the drill: Number 2 pencils, lined paper, a notebook, an eraser, and maybe a bottle of water. This is *your* training gear. Your puppy needs their own special collection to set them up for success. Here is a list of the basic supplies and what each one is used for.

COLLAR AND TAG: This is a collar, with an ID tag attached. It will feel weird to your puppy at first, but they'll get used to it quickly. The collar should be loose enough that you can slip a couple of fingers in between the collar and your puppy's neck, but not so loose that it can slip off.

LEASH: A good leash for your puppy is six feet long. Any leash with a comfortable handle is fine. But avoid all retractable leashes (the kind that roll up automatically)—they give a false sense of control and often cause serious injuries.

Leashes are important not only to keep your puppy close, but also to help your puppy pay attention to whatever you are doing. Without a leash, a puppy's natural curiosity will have them constantly wandering off to explore the universe.

FRONT-CLIP HARNESS: Here's our old friend, the front-clip harness (page 33). It should fit pretty snugly. They have adjustable straps. But they can only be adjusted so far. If you have a medium or large breed of dog, they will keep growing and will likely need at least one larger harness as they get older.

TRAINING TREATS: Positive training requires a lot of treats, but not all treats are the same. The best treats are entirely or mostly made out of meat. Almost any kind of meat is fine, like chicken, beef, and also "exotic" ones like alligator, bison, kangaroo, duck, lamb, and goat. Your puppy will enjoy a variety!

Treats need to be small, so that means either buying treats that come in tiny pieces or ones that can be easily torn into small pieces.

The kind of treat you *don't* want to use for training is dog biscuits. Biscuits are hard, crunchy, and crumbly. Timing matters when you're training, and biscuits take too long to chew and leave distracting crumbs on the ground.

TREAT POUCH: A treat pouch, also called a bait bag, is a container that you can clip to your pants or belt or wear across your body with a strap. It holds all your treats so that you're always ready to train and reward. If you don't have one, you can make one with a little bag and some sort of clip to attach it to your hip. A good treat pouch makes it easy to very quickly grab a treat without having to search around in your pocket.

CRATE: Your puppy's home-within-home is a cozy private fort called a crate (see page 24). Your puppy should be able to turn completely around inside and stretch out to lie down, but nothing bigger than that. Most crates are made out of metal or plastic. You don't want a fabric crate, because your puppy will chew it up.

PUPPY PEN: A pen is a foldable fence. Until your puppy is fully trained, a pen is a great way to limit your puppy's play space. It is perfectly okay for anyone to go inside the pen to play with puppy, unlike the crate.

Because pens fold, they are great to bring over to someone else's home. For example, imagine you are having Thanksgiving dinner at the home of a family member. By bringing the pen and setting it up, you can hang out with your family while your puppy roams around their pen.

If you are going to leave your puppy in the pen for a little while and you are worried they might have an accident, you can put pee pads on the floor.

PEE PADS: Pee pads are just like baby diapers, except they aren't worn—they lie flat on the floor. Like diapers, they can absorb a lot of liquid. Since puppies like to pee where they smell pee, many pads come with an attractive odor. The pads won't smell like anything to you, but your puppy will notice!

After your puppy uses a pad, it should be thrown in the trash right away and the area needs to be cleaned.

POOP BAG: Take one with you whenever puppy goes outside to go potty. They help keep your neighborhood clean. Picking up after your puppy is an important first step in being a responsible pet owner.

If you're concerned about the environment, there are lots of biodegradable and compostable poop bags you can buy.

CLICKER: This is a small device that you push with your thumb to make a clicking noise. Clickers are used in puppy training to let a puppy know they just did the right thing.

In this book, we are going to use the spoken word YES! instead of having you use a clicker. At the Zoom Room, we have seen a lot of kids play with the clicker and click it too much. Clicking all the time or at the wrong time can really confuse your puppy and make it harder for them to learn.

If you do have a clicker in your home, please do not play with it. If your grown-up is using a clicker to train your puppy, that is great. It won't matter at all if they are using a clicker and you are using YES!

How Do I Train My Puppy?

Now that you are ready to start training your puppy, you are going to be giving them lots of instructions. Training commands may be given to your puppy with hand gestures and words. When you teach your puppy, you will teach them both the gesture and the command word or phrase. Your puppy will learn the gesture first and the word second.

Training your puppy means keeping calm. Losing your patience will slow down puppy training. Worse, think of the fear phases. Your puppy could develop some behavior problems if they are afraid.

 TIP No one is perfect. If you find yourself losing your cool, the best thing you can do is ask a grown-up to help you out.

The type of training you're learning in this book is called *positive reward* or *positive reinforcement*. It is all about teaching your puppy that while you may be the boss, you are really their kind and generous leader.

When your puppy does something you love that they're supposed to do, say YES! and clap, laugh, and smile. Think of your voice and positivity as having the power to show your puppy what you want. In dog training, this is called *shaping*. The positive feedback increases the closer your puppy gets to performing the exact behavior desired.

A puppy's brain can only connect a reward to an action if they get the reward within two seconds of the action. Imagine you tell your puppy to sit and they sit. You dig around in your treat bag, get a treat, and take it over to your puppy. Your puppy has already seen you digging for goodies and hopped back to their feet, wagging their tail. Then you give your puppy their reward. About five seconds have passed since your puppy sat.

At the moment you give the treat, what is your puppy doing? Standing and wagging their tail. You have just taught your puppy how to stand and wag their tail, not to sit.

That won't work. What you really need is some kind of *bridge* that connects the correct behavior to the treat that will come a few seconds later.

THE POWER OF YES

Our bridge is the happily exclaimed word YES! When your puppy sits, you say YES! right away to praise their behavior. Then you can give the treat, even if it's a few seconds later.

You are using YES! as your bridge. It is what we call a *verbal marker*. It is a spoken response.

YES! is a powerful word in puppy training. It lets your puppy know they have done the exact right thing to make you happy. And it takes only a fraction of a second for you to say it.

Now we are going to teach your puppy what the word YES! means. Your puppy doesn't speak your language yet, so we need to teach them a simple definition:

YES! = Reward (Treat)

1. Sit in a chair near your puppy, holding a bag of about 20 treats.

2. Say YES! in a happy voice and then immediately give your puppy a treat.

3. Repeat this until your bag is empty: YES!/treat. YES!/treat.

We are not asking your puppy to perform any kind of trick or behavior. We are rewarding them for doing nothing.

This is language class. We are *Loading the Yes*. This means we are teaching your puppy to connect YES! with the deliciousness of tasty treats.

This is a powerful association for your puppy. Now, whenever you say YES! your puppy knows they did something wonderful because they have learned that a treat is sure to follow.

Puppies are puppies, and they don't always do what you want. So what is the opposite of YES?

In puppy training, the opposite of YES is actually *nothing*. It is silence.

Training your puppy means that when they do what you want, you quickly give a verbal marker (YES!) and then a reward and positive praise. And when your puppy does something you don't like, you ignore them.

By ignoring the thing you don't want your puppy to do, you will eventually *extinguish* that behavior. We usually say extinguish when we mean putting out a fire. You put out a fire by taking away its oxygen. Your happy feedback and praise is the oxygen your puppy wants. When you don't reward your puppy for something, your puppy will stop doing it.

Never say "No" or "Bad dog." Never punish or scold.

You might be wondering about that command we had you use earlier: AH AH. You used it when your puppy didn't perform the behavior quite the way you wanted. Isn't AH AH just another way to say "No"?

It is actually much different. It is what we call a *nonresponse marker.* You say it in a calm voice. It is simply a very short way to say, "Okay, I see that you're trying, but that is not exactly the answer I was looking for. Try again?"

We believe there is a big difference between "Not quite" and "No!"

Let's see if you can tell when to use the nonresponse marker AH AH with your puppy and when you should do nothing.

1. You walk into your room and find one of your stuffed animals was chewed up.
   a. Say AH AH
   b. Do nothing

2. You discover pee on the floor.
   a. Say AH AH
   b. Do nothing

3. You catch your puppy in the act of peeing on the floor.
   a. Say AH AH
   b. Do nothing

4. You're playing Touch and your puppy sniffs at your treat bag instead of your fist.
   a. Say AH AH
   b. Do nothing

5. You're teaching Sit and your puppy backs up instead of sitting down.
   a. Say AH AH
   b. Do Nothing

Answers:

1. *b) Next time, remember that your toys should be put away safely to prevent this.*

2. *b) Too much time has passed for your puppy to learn anything from saying AH AH.*

3. *a) And remember to then put on their leash and take them outside to finish.*

4. *a) Your puppy needs a gentle reminder to focus on your hand, not your treat bag.*

5. *a) This helps your puppy understand that backing up isn't what you're looking for.*

JACKPOTS

If your puppy is struggling with a task, once they finally nail it, give them three or four treats instead of one. When you give your puppy a bigger reward than they were expecting, that's called a *jackpot*.

Getting a jackpot is a really big deal to your puppy. A puppy who finally sits correctly and then gets a jackpot thinks, "Wow. This is amazing. I'd better pay attention and do this same exact thing the next time the kid asks me."

Jackpots are also a terrific way to end a training session. Puppies learn that training is fun and enjoyable when training ends with lots of treats.

PROOFING

You want your puppy to know that saying SIT means sit anytime and any-where that anyone says it. But if you taught your puppy to sit when you were in the living room and there was the sound of a truck coming from outside, your puppy possibly learned to sit when *you* said SIT in the *living room* with the *sound of a truck* nearby.

The next time you train, the truck isn't there, but your puppy still thinks SIT has something to do with you and with the living room. The truck lost its importance by going away. We need to do the same thing with the place (living room) and the trainer (you).

In dog training this is called *proofing*. Proofing means teaching a dog the same behavior in different situations, like outdoors instead of inside.

Proofing happens naturally over time. Soon, different family members will work on SIT, and they will happen to be in different places in and around your home.

Do not rush proofing. Before you are ready to proof the SIT, your puppy must be a total rock star at sitting every time you say SIT.

Once your puppy is getting it every time, the next time you work on SIT, try it in another room, outside, or with different distractions. And take turns with your family members so that other people are acting as the trainer.

LURING

Luring means using a treat in your hand to guide your puppy if they are struggling with a command.

Move your hand *slowly* when you lure. Keep your hand close enough to your puppy's nose so that they can lick your hand. And keep your fist closed around the goody so they can smell it but won't be able to take it from your hand.

Always remember that luring is positive, rewarding, and force free. You aren't touching your puppy. Never use your hands to try to push them into a sit or any other position. If you do that, your puppy won't learn and may start to avoid your hands.

A PUPPY'S ATTENTION SPAN

Puppies have very, very short attention spans. Most of the games we have played so far have only been two or three minutes long. That's plenty for a puppy. They are easily distracted.

Can your puppy really learn in just a few minutes? Yes and no. Yes, your puppy absolutely can learn, but only if you are training several times a day. If you only do a few minutes each day, that is not enough. Many very short training sessions are much better than one long one.

Unless you are proofing something or we told you to use some distractions, your puppy will always learn best when there are no distractions.

What counts as a distraction to your puppy? Someone talking on the phone in another room. Sounds of cooking in the kitchen. People walking or running by. Other animals. These are all distractions.

Believe it or not, a television show or video game is not distracting to your puppy. Your puppy blocks those sounds out. So if someone is watching TV in another room, that is fine.

TRY THIS: TEACH SIT

Let's put together everything we have learned about puppy training and teach your puppy one of the most important commands: SIT.

Before we jump in, do you know *why* we teach SIT? SIT isn't really about the sitting. Saying SIT really means to take a moment, be still, and pay attention.

1. Find a spot inside that is nice and quiet with no distractions. Get a bag of treats and ask a grown-up to supervise.

2. Take one treat in your hand and close your fist around it. Hold your hand in front of your puppy's nose. Make sure not to hold your hand too high or your puppy might try to jump up.

3. Say SIT as you move your hand slowly over your puppy's head in a straight line toward their tail. Remember to say SIT only once. It is important to move your hand slowly so that your puppy is trying to lick at the treat the entire time.

4. By luring them backward with the treat, your puppy has two choices: sit down or walk backward.

5. If your puppy sits, exclaim YES! right away and let them have the treat. Then give them lots of praise and affection. Be sure to reward your puppy even if they do what we call the "puppy sit," a goofy looking move that young puppies do with their legs sort of swung out to the side. For a puppy, this still counts as a good sit.

6. Most puppies will be so excited by the treat and the praise that they will stop the sit, which means they will stand up. If that happens, you are all set to repeat the above steps. But if your puppy is still sitting, take a few steps back and clap your hands as you call your puppy. Once they hop up and walk over to you, you have succeeded in resetting and are ready to repeat the steps. Keep practicing for about three minutes.

1. If your puppy jumps up for the treat or even raises their front paws off the ground, calmly say AH AH and bring your treat hand back to your side. Once your puppy has all four paws on the floor, go back to step 2.

2. If your puppy backs up instead of sitting, say AH AH, take back the treat, and go back to step 2. If your puppy is backing up, you may be moving your treat hand too quickly. Move more slowly next time.

3. The first time your puppy learns something new is always the hardest. Because there is extra difficulty, you will want to give your puppy a bigger reward. If your puppy has struggled with SIT, then finally gets it, instead of giving them one treat, give them three or four treats. Remember: This is called a jackpot. Training SIT is going to get a whole lot easier now.

4. Once your puppy has really mastered this, the next time you work on SIT, do it in a different room or with some distractions. Remember: This is called proofing.

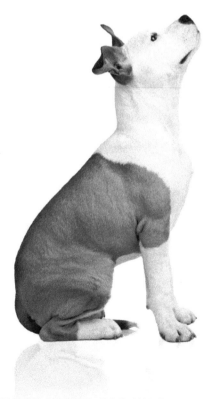

How Do I Motivate My Puppy?

Positive reinforcement puppy training, also called positive reward training, is as simple as rewarding your puppy when they do what you want them to do. But just what does your puppy find rewarding? Do you always have to give your puppy a treat?

Not at all. Sometimes a kind word is plenty. Other times simply getting to do what they want is the reward.

REWARDING WITH POSITIVE PRAISE

If you are not actually doing a training exercise to teach a new command or activity, but your puppy is doing something that makes you happy, be sure to praise them.

There is no magic word here. "Good girl" or "Good boy" is great. So is "I love you." Your puppy notices the tone of your voice and the delight in your face more than anything else.

Imagine that you are having dinner and your puppy is just lying on the floor quietly and not begging at the table. Tell your puppy they are doing a great job. Your puppy is learning that hanging out peacefully is a *desired behavior,* or something you want them to do.

If you get up from the table and give your puppy a treat, there is a good chance your puppy will stop sitting there nicely and will instead get up and follow you back to the table. Sometimes positive praise works much better than a treat!

SOMETIMES NO REWARD IS NEEDED

A lot of times, your puppy will ask you for something, and if you let them have it, that is their reward. If you are playing fetch and your puppy is sitting politely waiting for you to toss the ball instead of trying to grab it from your hand, this is good behavior. Why give a treat or even kind words? What your puppy wants is for you to toss the ball. Go ahead and toss it!

It is the same thing if your puppy waits at the door for you to open it so they can go outside and play or go potty. They are doing the right thing. Reward them by opening the door.

It sounds simple, but sometimes you can accidentally teach your dog to do the behavior you don't like. Imagine that you are sitting and reading a book when you hear your puppy scratch at the door because they want to go play. You are so focused on your book that you ignore your puppy. Then your puppy barks a little and then some more. Eventually, you get so distracted that you get up and let your puppy out. But here's what you actually just did: Your puppy just learned to bark and scratch loudly to go out and play. That is not what you were trying to teach them!

Here is a better way to teach your puppy the desired behavior. As you get to know them better, you may see your puppy is looking at the door and sitting quietly nearby. Go let your puppy out. You are rewarding your puppy for being quiet.

If you do not reward your puppy fast enough and they start barking, remember to stop their behavior by ignoring it. Sit calmly in the chair, but listen closely to your puppy.

At some point, your puppy will stop barking. As soon as they are quiet, jump up from the chair and take them out.

Once this happens a few times, your puppy will learn that sitting quietly by the door gets them what they want, and that barking does not.

REWARDING WITH TRAINING TREATS

We really like treat pouches because they remind us that training opportunities happen throughout the day, every day, and often when we don't expect them. By wearing your treats, they are always handy.

Treats are used whenever you are trying to help your puppy to learn something new. Learning new things is hard, and treats give your puppy tons of extra motivation. If you ask your puppy to do something especially hard, a jackpot of treats to reward them will really help your puppy learn.

Besides training sessions, you should give your puppy a treat anytime and every time they do something special and unexpected that took some real effort. Let's say that you are out on a nice walk and there's a chunk of old cheeseburger on the sidewalk. If your puppy walks right by it instead of stopping to drool over it, that was not easy for them to do. Exclaim YES! and then give your puppy a treat.

TIP It is also great for friends and even strangers to give treats to help with socializing your puppy, so your puppy learns that the world is a warm, friendly place.

You want to give your puppy lots of treats during training sessions and when they learn something very difficult. But giving your puppy too many treats can be unhealthy for them. Most of the time, positive praise or letting your puppy have what they waited patiently for is enough of a reward. If you are using teeny tiny meaty treats, not overfeeding, going on lots of little walks, and using lots of positive praise, you are doing everything right to help your puppy be healthy and happy.

WHAT ELSE MOTIVATES MY PUPPY?

Back when you learned Fetch (page 21), we asked you to take time to learn something about your puppy. Is your puppy a Fetch fanatic? Do they go bonkers for tennis balls? If so, you just stepped up your training game. Instead of reaching for a treat to reward your puppy, you can grab a ball and toss it.

What else might your puppy like? Some puppies are crazy about stuffed animals. At the Zoom Room, one of our most popular classes is agility training in which the dog (or puppy) runs through an obstacle course, weaving between poles, diving through a tire, jumping over hurdles, and traveling through winding tunnels.

Many people will use treats to lure their dog through the course. But over the years, we have seen lots of people use their dog's favorite stuffed animal and hold it in their hand, using the toy to motivate their dog.

Spend your first few weeks with your puppy learning what things they love. Here are some of the things and activities we have seen light up the faces of puppies:

» Fetching balls, flying discs, or other chew toys

» Tug-of-war

» Plush stuffed animals

» Car rides

- » Being brushed

- » Going for a walk

- » Swimming

- » Goofing and laughter

That last one I added for my own dog, Clyde. He is unusual because he does not have much of a prey drive. That means he does not like any toys or playing Fetch, and he is not even all that crazy about treats or food. But my son and I noticed that if we act silly, roar with laughter, and dance around like goofballs, Clyde lights right up and displays all the play gestures and signs of canine happiness. So we have actually used silliness as a motivator to train him.

Every puppy is unique, and you are now setting off on the great adventure of discovering what your own puppy loves the most.

TRY THIS: GIVE YOUR PUPPY POSITIVE MOTIVATION

For this exercise, all you have to do is make a wish list. Now that you know there are learning and training opportunities all around you all the time, think about the behaviors you want from your puppy.

What would you like your puppy to do? How might you reward your puppy when they do these things?

Make your wish list. Read it over a few times. That's it.

Now, the next time you see your puppy doing something on your list, you will know how important it is to jump right in with a joyous YES! and a reward. Depending on what it is, maybe you will use positive praise, maybe a treat, maybe your puppy will get the thing they want, or some other special thing that will delight them and help them understand how happy you are with what they're doing.

WHY DOES MY PUPPY DO THAT?

Puppies don't mean to cause problems, but they do like to play. And sometimes this play can look a lot like naughty behavior.

Imagine a class clown who keeps goofing off because they get attention. Puppies are the same way. Someone getting all worked up and having a huge reaction to something they did is really very interesting to a puppy. "I did this thing, and look at what I made that human do," they think. So they do it again.

If you know why your puppy acts the way they do, their behavior will be easier for you to understand and predict. This will help you stay patient and keep from getting frustrated with your puppy.

Negative attention is still attention. *Remember: To get rid of unwanted behaviors, extinguish them by ignoring them.*

Your puppy can become afraid of you if you lose your patience with them. Even worse, scolding a puppy will only reinforce the behavior that frustrated you. So when your puppy does something you don't like, go read a book, eat a snack, or call a friend. Do anything other than give your puppy attention.

Now, let's find out why your puppy misbehaves, so you can learn what to do instead of losing your cool.

Why Does My Puppy Lie on My Toys?

This bit of puppy mischief became the very first lesson in puppy training my son ever learned, back when he was really little. My son would pick a spot on the floor to build a Lego creation. No matter where he was, our dog Clyde would come over and lie down right on top of his masterpiece.

My son quickly learned the right thing to do. He would hide his frustration. Then he would walk to another spot, call Clyde over in a cheerful voice, and when Clyde bounded over, my son would have him lie down. He would then pet him, praise him, maybe give him a treat, and tell him what a good boy he was. Then my son would return to his toys.

There are three important things my son did. He did not get mad; he asked Clyde to do what he wanted; and he rewarded Clyde when he did the desired behavior. The big idea is that instead of telling your puppy what *not* to do, you tell them what you *do* want them to do.

Out of everywhere your puppy can go, why do they lie on your stuff? It's simple: Because they adore you! They are den animals, and they like physical closeness. Plus, they are naturally curious.

Let's make some other spot in your home even more special.

TRY THIS: TEACH YOUR PUPPY THE BOUNDARY STAY

You want your puppy to know that when they go to their special place, great things always happen. In dog training, this is called a *Boundary Stay*. You will teach your puppy to go to their bed on command (PLACE!) and stay there until you tell them it is okay to leave (FREE!).

PART 1: STANDING RIGHT NEXT TO THE BED

1. Ask a grown-up to help you find a good rug, blanket, or towel that you can use as a bed for your puppy (wait until your puppy gets older to use an actual dog bed; at this age, puppies will destroy them) and lay it out on the floor. Also ask them for treats, a bag, and supervision.

2. Stand next to the bed. With a treat in your hand, make a sweeping gesture with your arm to point at the bed while saying PLACE!

3. When your puppy comes over, as soon as at least three of their paws are on the bed, say YES! and then give them the treat.

4. Step away from the bed and clap your hands or slap your knees. When your puppy comes toward you, as soon as all four of their paws leave the bed, say FREE! But do *not* give a treat. FREE! is what we call a *release command*. When your puppy goes to the bed, they get a YES! and a treat, but their reward for leaving the bed is freedom.

5. Repeat steps 2 through 4 a few times.

6. Take a break. This training takes some time. It could take a few days or even a couple of weeks. Keep repeating steps 2 to 4 a few times each day. Once your puppy always goes to their bed when you make the sweeping gesture and say PLACE! you are ready for part 2.

PART 2: MOVING AWAY FROM THE BED

1. Take one step away from the bed and keep the treats in your pouch. Say PLACE! and make the sweeping gesture toward the bed.

2. When at least three of your puppy's paws are on the bed, say YES! and then give them a treat from your pouch.

3. Step a few feet away and call your puppy over. When all four paws are off the bed, say FREE!

4. Repeat steps 1 through 3 until your puppy has done it right about 10 times. The next time you train, stand two steps away.

5. Over the next week or two, keep practicing. Move a little farther away each time. If your puppy does not go, move a step closer and try again.

6. Once you can gesture from across the room, say PLACE! and always have your puppy run over to the bed, you are ready for part 3.

PART 3: LONGER STAYS

1. The final challenge is getting your puppy to stay on their bed until you release them. See if you can get your puppy to stay on their bed for 30 seconds. It doesn't matter if your puppy is standing, sitting, or lying down, as long as they are on the bed.

2. See if your puppy will stay for a minute. After 30 seconds, give them a treat but keep them on the bed for another 30 seconds. Then release them.

3. Try two minutes, giving a treat every 30 seconds.

4. Now, try two minutes but give a treat after one minute.

5. Keep practicing, but instead of using treats, sometimes give praise instead.

6. Finally, try for five minutes. Over time, give fewer treats. The goal is for your puppy to stay without needing any treats or praise.

 TIP Remember the importance of proofing. Let everyone practice this command with your puppy. You can also pick up the bed, move it to another location, then practice in the new place.

EVERYONE IN THEIR PLACE

There is another version of Boundary Stay training that a lot of families find super fun, especially at mealtimes.

1. Your puppy now has their own special place: their bed. Pick a seat in the same room to be your own special place. Everyone else in your family should pick their own special place, too.

2. When everyone, including your puppy, is in the room, shout PLACE! Everyone should dash over to their own special place and sit there.

3. Stay sitting. Just wait. Give it a minute or two. Then shout FREE! Everyone should jump up from their place.

4. Go ahead and celebrate together. Then do it again!

NEED HELP? TROUBLESHOOTING THE BOUNDARY STAY

1. If your puppy is having a hard time learning to stay in their bed, make the bed magical by tossing treats onto the bed for your puppy to discover. When they are on the bed finding and eating the treats, say PLACE! so they learn to associate the word with the bed.

2. If your puppy wanders off the bed before FREE! is said, say AH AH as soon as they step off. Then lure them back onto the bed with a treat and say PLACE! Then give a treat, and keep giving them tiny treats as long as they remain on the bed. This teaches them that the bed is the place they want to be.

Why Does My Puppy Bark?

Puppies bark for all kinds of reasons. It is one of the ways they communicate. Over time, you will learn to understand what some of those barks mean.

ATTENTION BARKING: If your puppy is barking at you, they probably want your attention. Do not give in to this. Barking is not a polite way to ask for attention, so the best thing you can do is extinguish this behavior by ignoring it.

ANGER BARKING: It is unlikely your puppy is angry. If your puppy is upset, you will also see Signs of Stress.

PLAY BARKING: You will probably notice one special bark that is especially high-pitched. That is a play bark, and your puppy will usually make Play Gestures, too.

ALERT BARKING: Most puppies will bark when someone is at your door or when they hear a strange, loud noise. That is what we call *alert barking*. Some puppies do it more than others. Alert barking is not a bad thing at all. Your puppy wants to watch over you and protect your home, and this is a terrific job for a pup!

NUISANCE BARKING: Nuisance barking is not something you want. That is when your puppy sits at the door or window and barks at every single person or animal who passes by.

TRY THIS: GET RID OF NUISANCE BARKING

Remember that example of the class clown? The first time your puppy starts barking their head off, they are testing you. They are waiting for some reaction. If you let your puppy out, play with your puppy, tell your puppy to be quiet, or yell at your puppy, you are giving your puppy some kind of reaction.

1. If your puppy is nuisance barking, don't give in. Walk away. Water the plants. But do not wander too far because you are not actually doing nothing. You are now doing something incredibly important: you are *remaining vigilant.* That means paying very close attention. To your puppy, it looks like you are watering the plants. But you are listening and waiting for the barking to stop.

2. When the barking stops, slowly count to two in your head, then spring into action. Be sure to wait two full seconds.

3. Go rub your puppy's belly. Scratch behind their ears, give them a treat, and tell them you love them. Give your puppy lots of rewards for doing absolutely nothing.

4. The next time your puppy is barking, wait for them to be quiet for five seconds before you reward them. Over time, work up to 10 or even 20 seconds of silence.

When your puppy barked, they learned that nothing happened. But when they were quiet, great things happened.

This is masterful puppy training at its best!

NEED HELP?

If you practice these steps and find that your puppy is still barking a lot, try counting more slowly in step 2. If you reward your puppy too quickly, they will think you were rewarding them for barking! By waiting a few seconds after they've quieted down, they learn that you like the quiet, not the noise that came right before.

If they are still barking their head off even when you use a slow count, this is a good time to talk to a grown-up about finding a professional dog trainer to help.

Why Does My Puppy Growl?

Like barking, growls can also have different meanings. But unlike barking, the majority of growls are warning signs that mean stay back.

KEEP YOUR DISTANCE

When a puppy is growling, the safe thing to do is keep your distance. This isn't a training opportunity. Don't wait for your puppy to stop growling then rush over and pet them. Simply back off.

A puppy who growls while eating feels threatened and is trying to warn you that if you come near, they may bite. They may think that you want to steal their food.

A puppy who growls while playing with a toy is doing the same thing. They don't want to even *think* about the idea that you might try to take away that toy.

While we don't want you to ever be afraid of your own puppy, because growling is what usually comes before biting, we want you to respect those growls as meaning you are standing too near.

Don't view growling as a bad thing. It's not something to be punished. Your puppy can't help the fact that they're feeling threatened. Your puppy simply wants to be left alone right now. It's okay. It will pass.

PLAY GROWLS

Almost all puppies also have a play growl. It usually comes out when they're having a really good time. In the middle of a tug-of-war game is a typical time when a puppy might play growl.

But here's the thing: We're experts at this stuff, and even we have a really hard time trying to explain how to tell the difference between a keep-your-distance growl and a play growl.

To be safe, you should treat all growls as warning signs unless a grown-up tells you that your puppy is just playing and there's nothing to worry about.

If you find yourself feeling afraid of your own puppy, or notice that they are regularly growling even when you've given them plenty of space and they aren't playing with another puppy, we recommend that you talk to a grown-up about finding a great dog trainer to help you with these displays of fear before they turn into fighting behavior.

Why Does My Puppy Beg and Whine?

Even though your puppy just ate, they might beg for more food because of their scavenger nature. Remember, while dogs are domesticated, they developed from wandering wild animals who didn't know when they would ever find another meal.

Unfortunately, this worrying about food will never go away. When your puppy is a five-year-old dog and has been fed regularly every single day, you might think, "Okay, by now they should know we're going to feed them—nothing to worry about." But they can't overcome their natural instinct, and puppies and full-grown dogs will always beg and whine on occasion.

WHINING IS PLAN A. Babies, before they can speak, will usually cry a lot. They might cry because they're hungry, or lonely, or need a diaper change. They cry out, and a caretaker comes along, hopefully figures out what they need, and helps them out.

Puppies are very similar. Like babies, they don't speak your language, so they rely on the limited vocabulary they have. Whining, as well as scratching and pawing, is their go-to cry when they want something.

Say your puppy wants to get out of the crate. They will whine to get you to open the door. Whining is their Plan A. If they whine and then you open the door, they learn that Plan A works. If you do this, they will continue to whine a lot more.

If they want to be fed, played with, walked, or they just need a little attention, they'll always start with Plan A. But you can break this habit. One way to think about puppy training is to say it is all about teaching your puppy Plan B, and that Plan B—the one you *want* them to choose—is better.

To use another example, let's say a dog who needs to go potty tries whining to get your attention (their Plan A). But you'd prefer Plan B—that your puppy rings the Potty Bell (page 30). Once they learn that whining doesn't succeed, but the Potty Bell does, you have successfully trained your puppy.

If you cave in to whining, it's really no different from a parent who gives in to a child throwing a tantrum. Can you picture a child who got what they wanted every time they threw a tantrum? Yikes! You don't want your puppy to be like that child!

TRY THIS: EXIT THE CRATE WITHOUT WHINING

Let's practice the technique of rewarding Plan B with the example of letting your puppy out of the crate.

1. Don't put your puppy in the crate just to practice this exercise. Wait for a time when your puppy is already in the crate. The room should be free from distractions.

2. At some point, your puppy will awaken in their crate, hear or smell you, and will want to come out and see you. They will start whining.

3. On the outside, don't do anything. But on the inside, pay close attention to your puppy.

4. No matter how much your puppy whines, scratches, or paws at the door, stay still. Wait for them to stop whining. That's when they realize that Plan A is not working. Your puppy will become quiet and may even lie down.

5. Wait for about five seconds of silence, then open the crate door and let your puppy out with a warm greeting, followed by some fun playtime. If you want, you can give your puppy a treat when they exit.

6. As you continue to practice this, increase the amount of time you wait before you open the crate. Try 10 seconds, then 20, and eventually work up to 30 seconds of quiet before you open the crate.

And that is how your puppy learns that Plan B always works, and that Plan A never does.

TIP Remember: It's important that everyone in your household follows the same rules. Imagine if some of your family waits for quiet and some of them give in to whining. This will be confusing for your puppy. It will hold them back from learning.

We think you'll be amazed how quickly your puppy is going to learn to lie quietly when they want to be let out of the crate. Keep showing your puppy how happy you are with their wise choice of Plan B.

NEED HELP?

If you practice the crate exercise but your puppy is still always whining to come out of the crate, here are a few tips:

1. If your puppy really has to go potty, they'll whine, so make sure you're giving your puppy plenty of regular potty breaks.

2. Try moving a little farther away from the crate and be sure to be completely silent.

3. In step 5, try counting more slowly. If you open the door too quickly, your puppy thinks you're rewarding the whining instead of the silence.

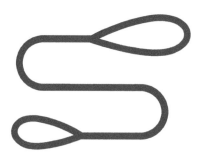

Why Does My Puppy Bite?

Even when they still have their puppy teeth, those are some extremely sharp teeth, and they are set in powerful jaws. Biting is a dog's primary method for defending itself.

Most people are very surprised to learn that 77 percent of dog bites come from the family dog or a friend's dog—not some wild scary animal roaming the streets.

The best way to avoid dog bites is to carefully study the Signs of Stress and to respect growling as a warning to keep your distance.

Nipping isn't the same as biting. A puppy that nips at your fingertips or ankles doesn't feel threatened and isn't trying to defend itself. In most cases, a nipping puppy is playing or teething. Also, certain breeds are born with a strong drive to nip.

Even though they're not the same as bites, nips still don't feel very good. Friends need to understand and respect each other's boundaries. Your puppy growls to ask you to respect their space. You need something like a growl to ask your puppy to respect your body.

TRY THIS: STOP YOUR PUPPY FROM NIPPING

If you are playing with your puppy, and they nip at your fingers or anywhere else on your body—even playfully—don't encourage and don't scold. The attention will lead to more nipping.

1. If your puppy nips at you, say AH AH and pull away the part of your body they were nipping.

2. Give your puppy a better choice for chewing, such as a chew toy.

3. If your puppy starts chewing the object you gave them, praise them. Then, enjoy some playtime with your puppy.

4. If your puppy goes right back to nipping you, say AH AH and walk away. No more playtime.

5. Puppies don't stay angry for long, and neither should you. Come back in a few minutes and play with your puppy again. Hopefully the nipping has stopped. If not, walk away again.

As with all of their training, your puppy should learn things pretty quickly. If you keep your cool and stick to the advice above, your puppy should stop nipping very soon.

NEED HELP?

TIP In step 2 of the anti-nipping exercise, it's important that your puppy feel like they are "trading up," or getting something better and tastier than nibbling on you. If your puppy isn't going for the chew toy, try a chewsicle (see page 72), a pig ear, a bully stick, or some other yummy chewable treat. If the nipping continues, tell a grown-up. If nipping doesn't stop, it is one of those situations in which the grown-up should seek out a good dog trainer in your area for help.

Why Does My Puppy Chew on Stuff?

Teething starts around the age of two months and lasts for a few months. You teethed when you were a baby, too. When adult teeth push out on baby or puppy teeth, it feels itchy and uncomfortable. Chewing on things feels good to teething puppies.

Adult dogs, long after they stop teething, also like to chew. Chewing is very pleasant to a puppy or dog. It keeps their attention and wakes up their brain. In this way, it's a bit like sucking on a thumb or pacifier, or biting fingernails.

Some humans like to chew gum in between meals instead of snacking. When you think about the importance of food and eating to a scavenger animal like a dog, you can appreciate why they enjoy chewing so much. Chewing is like pretend eating. A chewing puppy is working those jaw muscles, producing lots of saliva (drool).

Dogs also have a prey drive. Wild wolves will stalk prey and kill it with their mouth by biting. Domesticated dogs and puppies will chase a ball or other toy and act out the role of predator through play.

When a puppy bites on a stuffed bunny and shakes its head back and forth, it is going through the same motions its wild ancestor would have done with a real rabbit. But the puppy doesn't think it's attacking—puppies know they are playing, and they love it.

What your puppy does not know is which objects are okay to chew, and which ones are off limits. Teaching your puppy the difference is an important job for you.

Set your puppy up for success by keeping precious toys, shoes, and other off-limits objects out of your puppy's reach.

 TIP Tell a grown-up if you see your puppy chewing anything dangerous, such as electrical wires, or anything valuable to someone in your family.

YOU CHOOSE WHAT YOUR PUPPY CHEWS

Redirection—what magicians do—is your best bet when teaching your puppy what to chew. If your puppy has something that they shouldn't, remember to never try to take anything out of your puppy's mouth.

Instead, get your puppy's attention and give them a better and safer object to chew. Here are some good options:

» A chew toy

» A plush toy

» A rope toy (and an opportunity to play tug-of-war with you)

» A ball (if your puppy likes balls and you're up for a game of Fetch)

» A natural chew (bones, tendons, bully sticks, and other animal parts that grown-ups can purchase; some are even vegetarian, like sweet potato chews)

» A chewsicle (see below)

TRY THIS: MAKE A CHEWSICLE

What on earth is a chewsicle? Glad you asked! They're really fun to make, and you can have one or two always stored in your freezer, ready to use.

You will need a stuffable, hollow dog toy made of rubber or similar material. You'll stuff it full of deliciousness, toss it in the freezer until it is hard, and *voila*! You have made a chewsicle. It's that simple!

Try to come up with your own special recipes. Here are some good ingredients you can use:

» MEATS: Try using kibble, little bits of training treats, shredded or ground cooked chicken or turkey, or all the crumbs from the bottom of your treat pouch.

» FRUITS AND VEGETABLES: Try peas, carrots, zucchini, fresh parsley or mint, apples, bananas, dried cranberries, or shredded coconut.

» BINDER: A binder is something gooey that holds everything together and is great in chewsicles. Try peanut butter, yogurt, puréed sweet potato, mashed potatoes, cream cheese, or cooked rice.

» **SOAKED KIBBLE:** Instead of using a binder, you can soak kibble in either water or broth to make a good mush with which to hold everything together.

Chewsicles are not just tasty—they are real puzzles that take your puppy a long time to solve. Your puppy's brain, paws, and mouth will be working hard to figure out how to nudge and lick all the goodies out of the toy. Chewsicles will occupy your puppy for a long time.

NEED HELP?

If your puppy doesn't absolutely adore your first chewsicle recipe, it's okay; just try another recipe. Your puppy will like some food better than others, just like you! On your next try, go a little heavier on the meats. Be sure that all the pieces are nice and small.

You might find it fun and interesting to write down your chewiscle recipes in a journal as you invent and change them. That way, once you come up with a chewsicle recipe your puppy *really* loves, you'll easily be able to make it the the same way next time.

Why Does My Puppy Jump Up?

Jumping up can mean a couple of different things. Right now, we're going to talk about puppies jumping up on people, especially as a way of greeting. In the next section, we'll deal with puppies jumping up on furniture. In *both* situations, we're going to use the same training command: OFF!

TEACHING PROPER DOORWAY GREETINGS

Imagine walking in your front door, and your puppy jumps up to greet you. It feels like your puppy missed you so much and is so happy you're home.

There's plenty of truth to that, but remember: you are a puppy trainer now. Training a puppy means preparing for the future, helping your puppy grow up to be a wonderful, easy going, and well-mannered dog.

The cute little puppy jumping up today isn't going to be so cute when they are ten times bigger and knocking someone over! Even if you have a small breed, people aren't going to enjoy having their legs scratched up by that kind of greeting. Good habits start early.

So, even though a tiny puppy may be doing no harm today, today is when we teach your puppy that that is *not* how to greet someone. Your puppy will learn that greeting humans properly means always having *four on the floor.* In other words, the desired behavior in this situation is for the puppy to keep all four paws on the ground.

See how we turned it into a positive action? Instead of saying, *No, don't jump up*, we are saying, *Yes, do keep four on the floor.* When your puppy does the desired behavior, you reward it.

NO PUSHING

If your puppy jumps up and you push them down, you are breaking two of the main rules of positive training. First, you never use your hands to push your puppy into position. And second, your puppy will see your attention as a reward, even though it is negative attention (like that of the class clown).

Remember: the opposite of YES! is silence. It is turning your back and ignoring. And that is exactly how we train OFF!

TRY THIS: TEACH THE OFF! COMMAND

Make sure that everyone uses the same command: OFF! A lot of people might say "Down" when a puppy jumps up. But most people use the command Down to mean something totally different—it's the traditional command to tell a dog to lie down. Don't confuse your puppy by using the same word to mean two different things.

Unlike a command like SIT, which you can teach your puppy any time, for this one you're going to have to wait for the right opportunity. For now, learn the method and be prepared. You don't want to encourage your puppy to jump up on you just so you can teach them not to!

1. When your puppy jumps up on you, say OFF! once in an ordinary (not angry) tone of voice.

2. Immediately turn your back to your puppy. Your puppy no longer has your attention.

3. If there's a grown-up nearby, they can help by telling you the moment your puppy has stopped jumping and instead has four paws on the floor. If not, peek over your shoulder—try to be sneaky about it—to see if your puppy has calmed down.

4. As soon as they have four paws on the floor, turn around and praise your puppy and pet them a little. Don't give any treats—your attention is all they need.

With the OFF! exercise, don't go overboard with the affection or your puppy might get so excited that they start jumping again. If they do jump up again, start over at step 1. But this time, when you get to step 4, praise your puppy more calmly.

Why Does My Puppy Climb Furniture?

1. Puppies are curious and love exploring new places.

2. Puppies love to play. Leaping through the air and digging paws and noses into squishy surfaces is great fun.

3. Puppies like company, so wherever you happen to be, they'd love to join you.

4. Puppies adore smells. And nowhere in your house smells more like you than your bedsheets and any pillows or cushions where you lay your head—so the sofa, bed, or a reclining chair are treasured places where a puppy finds comfort, even when you're not in them.

All of those reasons are why your puppy climbs on the furniture.

Any other questions? Well, we have one suggestion. It's one you'll need to ask a grown-up. Ask which furniture your puppy is allowed on, and which is off-limits.

If the grown-up says the puppy is allowed to go anywhere they like, you can skip the rest of this section. But if they say that the bed, sofa, or anywhere else is a no-parking zone for puppies, then you should keep reading to learn how to train your puppy to stay off the furniture.

TRY THIS: KEEP YOUR PUPPY OFF THE FURNITURE

Let's pretend that a grown-up says that the living room sofa is off-limits. We'll show you what to do:

1. If you're now in the habit of always wearing a treat pouch full of treats since training opportunities can happen anytime and anywhere, that's great, and you're all set. If not, prepare for this training by hiding a little

baggie with tiny treats in an end table near the sofa so they'll be there when you need them.

2. Like the training in the last section (jumping up at the doorway), this is another one in which in order to teach it, you have to wait for your puppy to do the behavior that you don't want. Don't lure your puppy onto the sofa just so you can show them not to do that!

3. The next time you're sitting on the sofa and your puppy jumps up, give the non-response marker AH AH and reach for one of those hidden treats.

4. Stand up. Say OFF! and toss the treat to the ground, away from the sofa.

5. Say YES! as soon as your puppy jumps down to get the treat.

6. Go over to your puppy and reward them with praise and affection.

You have just taught your puppy that although climbing on the furniture to be with you is fun, there's far more enjoyment in paying attention to you when you say OFF!

NEED HELP?

In step 4, if your puppy doesn't jump down, it could be because they didn't notice the treat. Your puppy might still be up on the sofa, sniffing at your hand or trying to get to the pouch. If that happens, next time, take a *few* treats in hand and bring them near your puppy's nose to get their attention. Then toss them to the floor—but not too far away; your puppy should easily be able to see where you threw them. You can also try switching to a different treat—something really meaty that smells delicious.

Why Does My Puppy Bolt Out of the Door?

Curiosity and a love of exploration are wonderful qualities. They are also the reasons a puppy will bolt out of the door if it is left open.

There is little comfort in knowing your puppy is simply curious and not trying to escape if they run outside alone. A bolting puppy is headed for serious danger. We won't list all of the hazards—cars alone are bad enough.

We don't know if it's true or not, but kids get a pretty bad reputation when it comes to leaving doors open. So, many times, when we hear about a dog that ran away, the grown-ups say that a child accidentally left the door open. This is serious stuff and placing blame isn't the issue.

What matters is that now that you have a puppy, no one can ever leave the door open. Always assume your puppy will dash outside if the door is open.

 TIP You can also help by using puppy or baby gates. They keep your puppy in certain rooms and can prevent your puppy from being able to get to the door.

TRY THIS: PLAN AHEAD TO PREVENT BOLTING

Say a grown-up is on their way home from the store with a lot of bags and packages. When they get home, they'll need to make several trips back and forth, and they'd like to leave the front door open to make it easier to carry things inside.

» Here's how you can help by planning ahead. Before the grown-up makes the first trip inside, set up the pen and place your puppy inside. You just saved the day!

» No pen? No problem. Use puppy or baby gates to keep your puppy contained.

» No gates? It's fine. Put your puppy in their crate.

» Or, if the grown-up doesn't need any help carrying bags, you can simply put the leash on your puppy and hold on until the delivery is done and the door is closed.

Pen, gates, crate, or leash—it doesn't matter which one you use, as long as you think ahead to prevent your puppy from bolting.

Why Isn't My Puppy Paying Attention?

Have you ever been reading a book when your mind wanders off and you find yourself stuck on the same page? It's okay—we won't take it personally. It happens to everyone. The question is: *when* does it happen?

People and puppies have a harder time focusing when they feel sleepy, full, or nervous. They also have a difficult time paying attention when something else is far more exciting.

We believe you should always set your puppy up for success. If your puppy is exhausted, don't expect as much. Try not to ask anything of your puppy. Right after they've finished a meal is also a time to avoid training sessions.

Hunger, on the other hand, can be your friend. Right before mealtime, those treats in your bag are suddenly worth a whole lot more, and your puppy's focus will sharpen.

At school, your teachers probably don't jump out in the middle of recess and ask you to learn geometry. Likewise, if your puppy is having an absolute blast doing just about anything, let them have their fun. Yes, you might have some treats and a cool trick to teach them, but it's just not as interesting as that chewsicle they're gnawing on.

GETTING YOUR PUPPY'S ATTENTION

What if your puppy isn't tired, nervous, recently fed, or romping around, but they still seem to be ignoring you? Is there some way to win back your puppy's attention? Definitely. We can recommend three good games to use whenever you'd like your puppy to pay more attention to you.

Most of your teachers probably have similar games they play with you in school when they want everyone to settle down and listen. Some teachers use "1-2-3-Eyes-On-Me." Others use a musical instrument. Some simply put their hand up in the air until the whole class returns the gesture.

Our three games are very similar to those. Two of them you already know: the Name Game (see page 17), and Touch (see page 7), both in Chapter 1. Go back and play either of those games for a few minutes. Those are excellent ways to get your puppy's attention again.

Here's a third one, Watch Me, which you can practice any time you like.

TRY THIS: WATCH ME

1. Ask a grown-up to supervise, and for treats and a bag.

2. Place your puppy in a Sit, using the instructions from Chapter 3.

3. Take a treat and close your hand around it. Hold it near your puppy's nose so they can smell it.

4. Say WATCH ME! as you slowly raise your hand to the side of your face, then open your hand so they can both smell and see the treat.

5. When your puppy makes eye contact with you, say YES! and give the treat. Don't forget to say GENTLE if they are grabbing the treat too roughly.

6. Repeat the steps above three or four times so that your puppy is perfect at this.

7. Now repeat the steps again, but this time don't say YES! or give the treat until your puppy has maintained eye contact for five seconds.

8. Keep repeating this game, building up to ten seconds of eye contact before you give the reward.

 TIP Once your puppy knows Watch Me, you can give this command any time you'd like your puppy to pay attention to you. Just remember not to give the command when your puppy is unlikely to succeed, like when they're tired out or in the middle of a great playtime.

NEED HELP?

If your puppy isn't looking up at you, make sure that you're practicing in a room free from distractions. In step 3, make sure your puppy really got a good sniff so they know there's a treat in your hand. In step 4, if you move your hand too quickly, your puppy may lose track of the treat. But if you move your hand way too slowly, your puppy may get up and approach your hand, trying to get the treat. Our best advice is not to move on to step 7 until your puppy is an expert at Watch Me, then really take your time in building up longer and longer eye contact times.

GROWING UP
WITH MY PUPPY

Your puppy will only be a puppy for a pretty short time. Probably by the time you're in the next grade in school, your puppy will have grown into an adult dog.

But there are so many amazing activities you and your puppy can do together as both of you grow older. Places to go, people to see, games to play, tricks to learn.

We'd like to offer some suggestions about how you can continue to enjoy the company of your new best friend.

How Can We Stay Best Friends Forever?

Over the years to come, both you and your puppy will be going through changes. Your puppy will soon be a dog, and before you know it, you will be a teenager.

You've learned that being friends means understanding each other. Having almost finished this book, you're well on your way.

But being friends also means making time for each other and doing activities together. This will be your biggest challenge as friends and school and other interests take up more and more of your time as you get older.

So the best advice we can give you is to continue to make time for your furry best friend. Take great pride in introducing your puppy to your friends. Include your puppy in your activities and adventures.

The next section has some ideas about taking your puppy out around town.

Fun Activities as Your Puppy Grows Older

All of the knowledge you've learned about positive reward training for puppies will be equally useful for dog training.

You will no longer need to teach your dog the beginner stuff, like potty or crate training. But a whole new world of activities will open once your puppy knows the basics.

DOG SPORTS

Dogs can be incredible athletes, and there are many fun sporting events that you and your dog can take part in. You and your dog can learn how to play sports like these at the Zoom Room or another local training center or club.

» AGILITY TRAINING. This is one of our specialties at the Zoom Room. Your dog runs through an obstacle course that changes all the time—like jumping over hurdles and climbing ramps, or weaving between poles and diving through tunnels—all while you run alongside them, shouting commands and giving hand signals. We have found that all dogs can do great at agility training. We even offer agility for puppies! It's a terrific way to deepen communication between you and your dog while getting lots of exercise and having fun.

» FLYBALL. Your dog runs back and forth in a lane, doing spin turns at each end, as they chase a ball that gets launched each time they reach one of the two ends. Speed counts!

» TREIBBALL. We call this Urban Herding, as it's a lot like herding sheep, except it's indoors, and instead of sheep, you use big exercise balls which your dog herds into soccer goals. Herding breeds like shepherds and corgis have a real advantage, but no matter what kind of dog you have, this is a real test of your communication skills and your dog's obedience.

» EARTHDOG. Originally designed for dachshunds and small terriers, other dogs can participate, too. This tests your dog's digging and hunting abilities as they dig to try to find rodents (safely protected in cages).

» SKATEBOARDING/SURFING. You may have seen videos online of dogs riding surfboards and skateboards and having a blast. It's surprisingly easy to teach a dog to ride a skateboard; we include it in our Tricks workshops. Like all new behaviors, it's all about going slowly and taking baby steps until your dog has mastered it.

NOSEWORK

A dog's greatest ability is its amazing sense of smell. That's why dogs are so often used to search for missing people, to rescue them from a building, or to locate dangerous stuff like explosives. The same skills that can help a dog find a person or a bomb can also be used for more fun jobs around your home, like sniffing out a missing television remote control.

Scent or Nosework classes teach your dog to notice differences between special odors. We play all kinds of games to challenge your dog to find a tiny drop of the target scent that has been hidden among lots of objects.

ADVANCED OBEDIENCE TRAINING

Many people bring their dogs to obedience classes to help with skills like walking nicely on a leash or coming when called. But others continue on to more advanced types of obedience training.

» THERAPY DOG TRAINING. Therapy dogs are a wonderful way for you to share your dog's love and comfort with those who need it most. They always work as part of a team, meaning their human is always with them when they go out to help people, like visiting sick people in the hospital, or the elderly in a nursing home, or anyone who is going through something very sad or scary. Therapy dogs need to be extremely well trained so that they don't react to sudden movements, or to objects that might be unusual to them like wheelchairs or medical equipment. They usually know a bunch of fun tricks, too, to bring a smile to someone's face. You and your dog together must pass a very difficult test in order to become a therapy dog team.

» RALLY OBEDIENCE. This is a competition with lots of different stations, where you must give your dog specific commands at each one. It's a way of testing how well your dog listens as you try to get through the challenging course as quickly and as accurately as possible.

DOG TRICKS

There is really no limit to the kind of tricks a dog can do. You've probably seen dogs do all kinds of amazing things in movies, television shows, or on YouTube. The very first skill that all dogs need in order to perform tricks is the very first one we did in this book: TOUCH. If you think about it, when you got your dog to ring the Potty Bell (see page 30), that was kind of like a trick, and you did it by building up from the TOUCH command.

If you've ever learned a dance, you might remember that first you learned each of the steps, and then you learned to put them all together. Dogs learn complicated tricks the same way: first they learn each little piece, and then they learn to connect them together into one performance.

TRY THIS: TWIRL

Talking about tricks is one thing. We think it would be more fun to actually *do* a couple of tricks, so let's teach your puppy a trick right now called TWIRL.

1. You'll need treats, a bag, and a grown-up. Practice this indoors, in a room without any distractions.

2. Place your dog into a Sit position.

3. Hold a treat in your right hand and lift it a few inches above your puppy's nose. Your puppy should lift their front paws off the ground as they try to stretch up to reach it.

4. Say TWIRL! as you make a circle with your hand like you are stirring a pot with a magic wand.

5. You stir far enough to one side so that your puppy—still sitting up—turns their body to the side to face the treat.

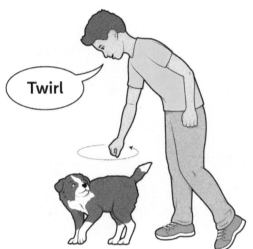

6. Then you continue stirring back toward their tail so that your puppy turns to face away from you toward the treat that was just behind them a moment ago.

7. Keep stirring to the other side, so that your puppy continues turning, and then back to where you started.

8. Give your puppy the treat and lots of praise.

9. Be sure to start this with slow hand motions. But once your puppy gets it, as you keep practicing, you should increase the speed.

10. After your puppy has successfully twirled about five times in a row, try the trick without a treat in your hand. Simply hold your hand in the position above their nose and make a quick stirring motion with your hand while exclaiming TWIRL!

11. If your puppy gets it, jackpot the treats. If not, go back to practicing with a treat in your hand.

How Can I Learn More about Dogs?

We've now come to the end of this book, but that doesn't mean it needs to be the end of your learning more about puppies and dogs.

PUPPY S.T.A.R.

One of the very best ways to learn more is to help your puppy achieve Puppy S.T.A.R. status. S.T.A.R. stands for Socialization, Training, Activity, and Responsibility. It's a special program run by the American Kennel Club.

You can find a link in the Resources section (see page 91) to learn more about the program. One of the steps needed to pass is by taking six training classes with your puppy. We'd definitely encourage you to go to these classes with your puppy—it's a great way to learn more.

YOUTH ORGANIZATIONS

The Girl Scouts of America and other youth organizations offer Pet Care badges. If you take part in this or a similar youth group, ask your troop leader for more information about activities you can do to earn these badges.

DOG DOCUMENTARIES

There are some wonderful movies and television series that you can watch with your whole family to learn more about dogs. Here are some of our favorites:

» *Dogs with Jobs*

» *The Secret Life of the Dog*

» *And Man Created Dog*

» *Dogs Decoded*

» *Dogs* (6-part series on Netflix)

» *A Dog's Life*

» *Through a Dog's Eyes*

VOLUNTEERING

In your town there are probably a lot of animal rescue groups that hold adoption fairs. Ask a grown-up if you can volunteer to help out at the next one.

There are many careers for dog lovers. These include veterinarians and vet techs, dog trainers, dog walkers, dog sitters, shelter workers, dog groomers, and more.

If you're interested in these careers, ask a grown-up to help you find a local business where you might be able to volunteer or do a summer internship. Even if it turns out you're too young now, at least you'll find out more about what you need to do to prepare for a learning experience like that. If your school has a Career Day, talk to your teacher and ask if they can invite one of these dog professionals.

RESOURCES

American Kennel Club's Guide to dog breeds: AKC.org/dog-breeds

American Kennel Club S.T.A.R. Puppy Program: AKC.org
/products-services/training-programs/canine-good-citizen
/akc-star-puppy

Dog-centered meet-up groups: MeetUp.com/find/?keywords=dog

Dog-friendly places from Yelp.com: Yelp.com/search?find_desc
=%22dog+friendly&attrs=DogsAllowed

Dog-friendly places from BringFido.com: BringFido.com/attraction

Dog Safety for Kids: TheFamilyDog.com/stop-the-77

List of plants toxic to dogs: ASPCA.org/pet-care/animal-poison
-control/toxic-and-non-toxic-plants?field_toxicity_value
%5B%5D=01

List of human foods poisonous to dogs: ASPCA.org/pet-care/animal
-poison-control/people-foods-avoid-feeding-your-pets

Tips on health, nutrition, and more from the Whole Dog Journal:
Whole-Dog-Journal.com

Zoom Room Guide to Dog Body Language: ZoomRoom.com/admin
/guide-to-dog-body-language

Zoom Room Guide to Dog Play Gestures: ZoomRoom.com/admin
/guide-to-dog-play-gestures

Zoom Room locations near you: ZoomRoom.com/locations

INDEX

ACKNOWLEDGMENTS

THIS BOOK WAS MADE POSSIBLE due to the generous contributions and advice of Liz Claflin, Zoom Room's Director of Operations.

My son, Meyer, also deserves thanks, as he read each chapter as soon as I finished writing it and gave me some great feedback.

I'd also like to warmly thank our dog, Clyde Orange, who has served as the Zoom Room's unofficial mascot for the past thirteen years. You were a perfect puppy and have grown to be a truly majestic beast, Clyde. You have brought smiles to countless faces, and unconditional love to my son and me. We love and laugh better because of you.

ABOUT THE AUTHOR

MARK VAN WYE is the CEO of Zoom Room, an indoor dog training gym with locations across the United States and more on the way. Founded in 2007, Zoom Room has made more than 150,000 tails wag. All Zoom Room trainers complete their own intensive training program, deeply rooted in the scientific literature of animal behavior and the practice of positive reinforcement. Mark has been with the company since its inception.

Mark grew up in Miami Beach and graduated from Amherst College, where he majored in neuroscience and English, and has an MFA in writing from Smith College. He has worked for decades in education as a teacher, writer, and curriculum creator, building afterschool programs for the Boys and Girls Clubs of America, and consulting on educational projects for clients such as Disney, Nintendo, and a variety of kids' educational television shows focusing on science.

Mark lives in Marina del Rey, California, with his komondor, Clyde Orange, and his son, Meyer. Both have been raised at the Zoom Room. Clyde has learned everything from obedience to agility to therapy dog training. And Meyer has learned about customer service, entrepreneurship, and animal behavior—and has also had most of his birthday parties there.

Mark and Meyer can frequently be seen walking Clyde around Venice, California, wearing matching Zoom Room shirts emblazoned with "Love. Unconditionally." (Mark and Meyer wear the shirts, that is. Clyde's unusual corded coat is all he ever needs to wear.)

9 781646 118656